S. Hrg. 114–608

MILITARY SPACE LAUNCH AND THE USE OF RUSSIAN–MADE ROCKET ENGINES

HEARING

BEFORE THE

COMMITTEE ON ARMED SERVICES
UNITED STATES SENATE

ONE HUNDRED FOURTEENTH CONGRESS

SECOND SESSION

JANUARY 27, 2016

Printed for the use of the Committee on Armed Services

Available via the World Wide Web: http://www.fdsys.gov/

U.S. GOVERNMENT PUBLISHING OFFICE

25–116 PDF　　　　WASHINGTON : 2017

For sale by the Superintendent of Documents, U.S. Government Publishing Office
Internet: bookstore.gpo.gov　Phone: toll free (866) 512–1800; DC area (202) 512–1800
Fax: (202) 512–2104　Mail: Stop IDCC, Washington, DC 20402–0001

CONTENTS

(III)

MILITARY SPACE LAUNCH AND THE USE OF RUSSIAN–MADE ROCKET ENGINES

WEDNESDAY, JANUARY 27, 2016

U.S. SENATE,
COMMITTEE ON ARMED SERVICES,
Washington, DC.

The committee met, pursuant to notice, at 9:30 a.m. in Room SH–216, Hart Senate Office Building, Senator John McCain (chairman) presiding.

Committee members present: Senators McCain, Sessions, Ayotte, Fischer, Cotton, Rounds, Ernst, Tillis, Sullivan, Lee, Reed, Manchin, Shaheen, Gillibrand, Blumenthal, Donnelly, Hirono, King, and Heinrich.

OPENING STATEMENT OF SENATOR JOHN McCAIN, CHAIRMAN

Chairman McCAIN. Good morning.

The committee meets today to receive testimony on military space launch and the use of Russian-made rocket engines from Under Secretary of Defense for Acquisition, Technology and Logistics Frank Kendall and Secretary of the Air Force Deborah James. We thank the witnesses for their service and for appearing before the committee.

With Russia and China aggressively weaponizing space, we can no longer take for granted the relative peace we have enjoyed in space for nearly 60 years. Both Russia and China are pursuing unprecedented counter-space programs and investing robust resources to challenge United States superiority in space. As Secretary James explained to "60 Minutes" last April, Russia and China are testing and investing in anti-satellite weapons, including direct assent missiles, ground-based lasers, and satellite jammers. To respond to these provocations, the Defense Department is investing $5 billion and reviewing nearly every facet of the way we operate in space and utilize our space-based capabilities.

In stark contrast to the reviews underway for satellites already in space, the Department appears less interested in rapidly addressing our most immediate threat, our reliance on Russian-made rocket engines. Today Russia holds many of our most precious national security satellites at risk before they ever get off the ground. Yet the Department of Defense has actively sought to undermine, with the support of the United Launch Alliance, ULA, and the parochial motivations of Senator Shelby and Senator Durbin, the direction of this committee to limit that risk and end the use of the Russian-made RD–180 by the end of this decade.

My views on this matter are well known. The benefits to Vladimir Putin, his network of corruption, and the Russian military industrial complex are also well known. Yet despite the availability of alternatives, a select few still want to prolong our dependence on Russia while they target our satellites, occupy Crimea, destabilize Ukraine, bolster Assad in Syria, send weapons to Iran, and violate the 1987 Intermediate Range Nuclear Forces Treaty.

Our hearing today will closely evaluate the arguments of those making the same empty promises and proposing the same gradual transition that had been promised since the Department of Defense first allowed the use of Russian-made engines in 1995. Even then, Secretary of Defense Bill Perry recognized the inherent risks and made domestic production within 4 years a condition for using the RD–180. That was back in 1995. Yet 20 years later, after numerous stalling efforts rooted in corporate greed and naive assertions of defense cooperation with Russia, little progress has been made in limiting the influence of Russia on space launch. This is unacceptable. I will do everything in my power to prohibit the use of Russian-made rocket engines in the future.

This committee has debated this issue at length. In hearings, in markup, and on the Senate floor, not once but twice. The Fiscal Year 2016 National Defense Authorization Act [NDAA] included compromise language that facilitates competition by allowing for nine Russian rocket engines to be used as the incumbent space launch provider transitions its launch vehicles to non-Russian propulsion systems. I certainly did not get the immediate prohibition I would have otherwise wanted, but was willing to compromise to send a unified message that the continued use of Russian technology to launch our satellites, not to mention the continued subsidy to Putin's military and close friends, was not in our national security interests.

At every turn, the Air Force and ULA [United Launch Alliance] have replied with stalling tactics, stale arguments, and suspect assertions. After years of reaping the benefits as a monopoly provider of space launch capabilities, ULA complains that eliminating the RD–180 will somehow result in replacing one monopoly for another. The fact is that ULA has two launch vehicles, and if the Air Force were to pursue split buys for a short period of time until a new engine is developed, we could eliminate our dependence on the RD–180 today without compromising future competition.

The Air Force has also complained time and again that it cannot develop a new rocket engine by 2019. It says an awful lot about the current acquisition system when the default assertion from the Air Force is that it takes longer to develop a rocket engine today than it took to develop the entire Saturn V launch vehicle that took us to the moon in the 1960s.

It is unfortunate that it took the threat of today's hearing for the Air Force to award a contract for a prototype to replace the RD–180. 2 years after Russia invaded Crimea, the Pentagon just recently signaled its desire to allocate over $250 million for a prototype replacement engine. Even this welcome gesture appears fraught with non-compliance to congressional direction. Instead of picking two promising designs, the Air Force appears poised to dilute the limited resources across numerous concepts, some of which would require the development of an entirely new launch vehicle. In doing so, they will all but guarantee that no one will be able to develop an engine to replace the RD–180 by 2019.

ULA appears to be willing to take whatever steps necessary to extend its questionable dealings with Russia. We saw this most recently when ULA took steps to manufacture a crisis by artificially diminishing the stockpile of engines they purchased prior to the Russian invasion of Crimea. That crisis proved short-lived. Just days after the signing of the omnibus appropriations bill, ULA announced it had ordered 20 new RD–180s, a nearly half a billion dollar windfall for Putin and the Russian military industrial complex with the added benefit of stringing out our dependence on Russian-made rocket engines. We must label ULA's behavior for the manipulative extortion that it is. I look forward to hearing from our witnesses today whether they support the actions ULA took when they sought to coerce a change in the law by not competing for the GPS III launch late last year.

Tomorrow I will be introducing legislation with House Majority Leader Kevin McCarthy to strike language air-dropped into the 2,000-page omnibus bill last month. This legislation is the first of many actions I will take this year to ensure we end our dependence on Russian rocket engines and stop subsidizing Vladimir Putin and his gang of corrupt cronies.

I thank the witnesses again for appearing before the committee, and I look forward to their testimony.

By the way, I did not mention the unprecedented and outrageous $800 million a year that ULA is paid for doing nothing, an unusual and incredible expenditure of taxpayers? dollars, which fortunately we have cut off as a result of this year's defense authorization bill.

Senator Reed?

STATEMENT OF SENATOR JACK REED

Senator REED. Thank you very much, Mr. Chairman, and let me thank you also for holding this hearing. It is a very important and vital subject.

I thank the witnesses for appearing and also for their service to the Nation in many different capacities.

I believe that today's hearing has three issues that the committee needs to understand and follow up.

First, what are we doing to develop a replacement for the Russian RD–180 engine? This committee has spoken forcefully, as the chairman pointed out, in two National Defense Authorization Acts to fund a replacement for it by 2019. The Congress has appropriated $444 million in the past 2 years in support of this effort, $304 million, indeed, that was above the sum requested by the Department of Defense. This is one of the rare events where the Department is getting substantially more funding than they are proposing. I believe we are sending a strong message, and we want your response.

Second, I believe we need to understand what the Department actually needs in terms of RD–180 engines based upon what current Atlas V rocket can uniquely lift that other competitors cannot currently lift. We have been told that Atlas V will operate through 2022 until a new rocket with a U.S. engine can replace it.

Third, I think we need to understand what the Department is doing to encourage the entrance of other competitors to the DOD launch market. The United Launch Alliance, or ULA, has to build an entirely new rocket. We should be encouraging other entrants as a hedge so that we avoid SpaceX being the only provider of launch, much like ULA was. In case there are delays with the replacement to this Atlas V rocket, we do not want to be in that position.

With that, let me thank everyone for their participation today, and I look forward to a very important hearing.

Thank you, Mr. Chairman.

Chairman MCCAIN. Welcome, witnesses. Secretary James?

STATEMENT OF HONORABLE DEBORAH LEE JAMES, SECRETARY OF THE AIR FORCE

Ms. JAMES. Thank you, Chairman McCain, Senator Reed, and other members of the committee.

Frank Kendall and I welcome the opportunity to provide our perspectives today on space launch.

The U.S. relies upon space as an essential element of our national security. Space provides us with the ability to operate effectively around the world, to understand what our own forces are doing, and to stay ahead of our adversaries. Space is key to projecting credible and effective power around the world to support our allies and deter aggression. Maintaining our advantage requires the ability to modernize and replenish our space architecture through a reliable launch capability. For this reason, maintaining assured access to space remains our number one priority. Indeed, this is memorialized in title 10 U.S. Code.

You may recall a string of launch failures in the late 1990s that resulted in the loss of billions of dollars of hardware and launches were suspended at that time for nearly 8 months while investigations were conducted. This experience reinforced the importance of having multiple pathways to space. Two highly reliable launch systems protect the Nation's ability to access space, if one system were to suffer a failure that grounded an entire fleet.

Assured access by law needs to be provided by U.S. commercial providers where space transportation services are required. Moreover, all of us—all of us—want competition between launch service providers because competition which, by the way, is also required by law, can help to control costs to the taxpayer and spur innovation in launch technology.

While we continue to believe that having access to about 18 RD–180s is prudent over the next few years to maintain competition in the short term, we also recognize very strongly the requirement in the fiscal year 2016 NDAA to transition away from the use of Russian engines through full and open competition. I assure you we are working all of these mandates in law as quickly as possible.

Now, this is an exciting time to be in space launch. Whereas in the 1960s and 1970s, Government investment largely drove technology development in this field, today private sources of funding have joined forces to spur a new generation of innovation in launch capabilities. That is a great deal for the taxpayer because it means that not all of the funding for these endeavors has to come from us the way it did in the 1960s and 1970s.

We are optimistic about these new commercial entrants and have contributed our time, resources, energy, and expertise to help develop their systems, understand needs, certify them for Government applications, learn from their failures, and celebrate their successes.

For example, I recently spoke with Elon Musk to congratulate him on the achievement of returning a first-stage rocket to earth in a controlled manner, which is an event that may someday allow reuse of a major rocket component and reduce cost to the U.S. taxpayer, as well as other customers. So we look forward to continue working with U.S. companies to help mature these capabilities.

In the meantime, however, we must keep in mind the only launch vehicles that can reach the full range of orbits and carry our heaviest payloads today remain the Atlas and Delta families. ULA builds and flies the Atlas and Delta for the U.S. Government and other commercial customers, and they currently enjoy an unprecedented record of successful launches, 90 of which were accomplished under the EELV program.

Now, this achievement was enabled by very high levels of mission assurance, including rigorous engineering review and component testing. Funding for these government-mandated mission assurance requirements, along with the costs of maintaining launch infrastructure and a skilled workforce, came through a contract vehicle with the government known as the EELV Launch Capability Arrangement, otherwise known as the ELC.

Now, while ULA operated in a sole-source environment, the ELC was an effective way to cover the government-mandated costs for the EELV, particularly the block buy. In a competitive environment, however, it is being phased out, just as the NDAA says, and it certainly will not be necessary in the future because we are moving into a world of competition.

In the interim, we have put in place an apples-to-apples cost adjustment situation for launch competitions to ensure fairness in those competitions.

Now, like some of you—perhaps all of you—I was very surprised and disappointed when ULA did not bid on a recent GPS competitive launch opportunity. Given the fact that there are taxpayer dollars involved with this ELC arrangement I just described to you, I have asked my legal team to review what could be done about this. They are looking at options, including early termination of the ELC arrangement and how such an early termination could possibly impact the repricing of remaining block buy launches.

Another complication to consider is the state of play on the Delta, which is no longer commercially competitive. Given the restrictions on the use of Atlas, DOD must look for ways to meet the mandate of at least two commercially viable launch vehicles or family of launch vehicles capable of launching national security payloads.

In a global launch environment, commercial viability is all about cost. How do you incentivize industry to make the investments needed to spur the innovation that will bring down those costs? Well, we decided to ask industry that question directly, which is why we issued an RFI and obtained data to address that matter about a year and a half ago.

Now, after studying the responses to this RFI, we selected public-private partnership as the best way to ensure access to at least two domestic launch service providers. This business model, I want to say again, is a better deal for the taxpayer because it uses to a degree other people's money to help eliminate our dependency on the RD–180. Our fiscal year 2017 budget request will reflect this approach.

Now, let me give you an update on our plan and our progress to date.

Our plan includes first implementing robust risk reduction and technology maturation efforts. The science involved with rocket launch and getting into space is hard science, and technology maturation and risk reduction is a good first step for hard science problems.

The second step is we are using other transaction authority agreements to execute fast and flexible teaming arrangements with industry partners for launch system development. While we expected that some rocket propulsion system work might be required within these agreements, we never intended to focus solely on rocket engines. Unfortunately, the NDAA limits our effort in fiscal year 2016 to development of rocket engines. Of course, we are complying with this requirement. The Department, however, would strongly prefer not to fund a rocket engine alone because a rocket alone will not get us to space. We need an entire capability, not just one single component. If we were to continue down the path of funding rocket engines alone, we believe this effort would benefit only one—only one—launch service provider, which we do not really believe is anyone's intent.

In fiscal year 2017, we need and intend to apply our investment to ensure the availability of a complete launch system through public-private partnerships. This in fact is step three of the plan.

Finally, in step four, we will award contracts for launch services projected to occur in the fiscal year 2022 and 2023 time frame. We believe this is the best approach to achieve our mandate of assured access to space with two certified commercially competitive domestic launch providers.

Implementing the fiscal year 2017 elements of this plan will require the removal of language that restricts the use of these funds to engine development alone, and we would greatly appreciate this committee's support of this approach. So far, of the $260 million authorized and appropriated, which is $41 million that was reprogrammed in fiscal year 2014 and $220 million authorized and appropriated in fiscal year 2015, we have obligated just over $176 million, which is all of the 2014 money that was reprogrammed and $135 million of the fiscal year 2015 dollars. The balance will be obligated soon pending, of course, successful outcome on negotiations with industry. All of these monies are directed toward the first two components of the plan that I just described to you.

To summarize, Mr. Chairman, we remain committed to assured access to space through at least two commercially viable domestic launch providers. We believe in competition. We think this is in the best interest of the taxpayer, and it ultimately will contribute to a healthy industrial base in the future over time.

We affirm we are moving as quickly as we can to eliminate the use of the RD–180 engine, consistent with the NDAA.

Finally, we remain committed to maintaining full compliance with sanctions against Russia. Yesterday I asked the Under Secretary for Policy and the General Counsel of DOD to work with our colleagues in the Departments of State, Commerce, and Treasury to update a previous ruling on the matter of Energomosh, given that there have been recent changes over the last few weeks in the management of the Russian space sector. We will get back to you on this soonest.

I thank you. I would yield to Mr. Kendall, and we look forward to your questions.

[The joint prepared statement of Ms. James and Mr. Kendall follows:]

JOINT PREPARED STATEMENT BY THE HONORABLE DEBORAH LEE JAMES AND THE HONORABLE FRANK KENDALL III

Chairman McCain, Ranking Member Reed, and distinguished Members of the committee, thank you for the opportunity to appear before you to discuss how we deliver national security space capabilities to the nation's warfighters and intelligence community (IC). These capabilities provide our nation decisive advantage in situational awareness, precision navigation and targeting, and command and control, and without assured access to space via reliable launch services, that advantage would be at risk.

Combatant commanders rely on space-based effects, including worldwide precision navigation, threat warning, protected strategic and tactical communications, for every military operation. Launch systems must provide assured access to space to ensure the benefits of space for military operations, diplomatic engagements, and the continued development of the economy. The loss of access to space would have an immediate and devastating impact on Department operations. Consequently, in today's increasingly contested space domain, the Department cannot depend entirely on only one source for critical national security satellites.

By way of background, the Department is both guided and constrained by public law in how we develop, sustain, and acquire national security space launch capability. The Department's number one priority in space launch is assured access to space, as codified in title 10, section 2273 of the US Code and the National Space Transportation Policy. Assured access to space as mandated by title 10 requires "the availability of at least two space launch vehicles (or families of space launch vehicles) capable of delivering into space any payload designated by the Secretary of Defense or the Director of National Intelligence as a national security payload." Ultimately, this law allows for continued access to space should one system suffer a fleet-grounding event or otherwise become unavailable.

The Department utilizes commercial space transportation services to meet its requirements, as mandated by the Commercial Space Act (51 U.S.C. 50131) and currently procures launch services for National Security Space launches. The Department does not take ownership of any launch hardware and plans to continue using the launch service approach to manage the transition from use of the RD–180.

HISTORICAL SIGNIFICANCE AND GETTING TO WHERE WE ARE TODAY

In the early days of U.S. space exploration, Government intellect and investment drove the development of launch capability it its entirety. The Gemini and Apollo programs in particular required systems with both the scale necessary for large payloads and the mission assurance standards for manned spaceflight. Industry provided significant contributions through cooperative research and development agreements as well as direct investment through traditional contracts, but the Government was the prime integrator, and owned the design and the key technologies developed for heavy launch. This arrangement—where any changes driven by the payloads rippled through the designs of the rocket propulsion system and the rocket itself, and the Government covered all of the costs—persisted until the Nixon Administration's decision in 1972 to merge the launch efforts of the U.S. Government for defense, scientific, and commercial purposes in a single Space Transportation System (STS). A primary goal of the STS, or Space Shuttle, was to obtain cost efficiencies across the Federal Government through sustained launch rates of mostly reusable hardware.

Tomorrow marks the 30th anniversary of the Space Shuttle Challenger accident. Many of us remember exactly where we were on that cold January morning in 1986 when the nation mourned the loss of seven brave astronauts. In the wake of Challenger, the Air Force modernized its expendable launch vehicle families—Atlas, Delta, and Titan—to launch critical national security payloads that would be grounded until the Space Shuttle returned to flight. The last years of the 1980s and the early years of the 1990s were spent launching these national security payloads on expendable launchers—as well as some remaining Space Shuttle launches—to meet the Department's growing need for space systems such as Global Positioning System (GPS) and Defense Support Program theater missile warning as demonstrated by their groundbreaking use during Operation DESERT STORM in 1991.

By the mid-1990s, the Department settled upon the Evolved Expendable Launch Vehicle (EELV) program as the path to establishing assured access to space. A large commercial launch market for commercial telecommunications satellites was expected to sustain the marketplace for multiple domestic U.S. launch vehicle providers so that the Federal Government could leverage economies of scale in a market-driven cost environment, and sustain alternatives should one launch vehicle family be grounded for any reason. At this juncture, The Boeing Company (Boeing) and Lockheed Martin Corporation (Lockheed Martin) were our two sources of launch capability in this class, but two events occurred that changed the landscape. First, a series of launch failures resulted in the loss of three national security payloads and more than $5.0 billion worth of hardware. The resultant failure investigations halted launch operations for nearly eight months, and reinforced the importance of access to multiple pathways to space.

Second, the commercial market did not materialize as predicted. To preserve the U.S. Government's assured access to space, in 2006 the U.S. Government supported the establishment of United Launch Alliance, a joint venture of Lockheed Martin and Boeing that combined the production of the Government space launch services of the two companies into one central plant, and co-located engineering functions to improve cost efficiency.

Since 2006, much has changed within the launch industry and the global security environment. New sources of domestic supply, such as Space Exploration Technologies (SpaceX), have successfully demonstrated their ability to deliver payloads into space. New arrangements between government and industry, as witnessed by NASA's Commercial Orbital Transportation Services (COTS) and Commercial Resupply Services (CRS) contracts with Orbital Sciences (now Orbital ATK) and SpaceX, have shown that innovative public-private partnerships can be leveraged to obtain reliable space launch services at reasonable costs. New commercial applications of space, including large constellations in low earth orbit for persistent remote sensing and global internet services, are driving growth in projected launch demand. Finally, growing concerns with the acceptability and availability of Russian-supplied engines in the wake of the 2014 Crimean crisis have called into question the United States Government's previous strategy of utilizing Russian RD–180 rocket engines for national security missions. Our strategy, in the early 2000s was to manufacture RD–180 engines for national security missions in the United States. We deferred co-production and ultimately moved towards a two-year stockpile of engines to mitigate disruptions to the supply chain. We are all in agreement with the need to end the use of the RD–180 with minimal impacts to national security as soon as possible.

COMPETITION AND NEW ENTRANTS

As noted, competition between launch service providers both complies with the terms of the Commercial Space Act and serves as a way of controlling cost and spurring innovation. While government investment has traditionally driven technology development in this field, private sources of funding have now joined forces to spur a new generation of innovation in launch capabilities.

We remain optimistic about these new entrants to the market, and have contributed significant time, energy and expertise to help them develop their systems, understand customer needs, certify them for government applications, learn from their failures, and celebrate their successes. We look forward to working with these companies to continue to mature their capabilities. In the meantime, we remain dependent on the Atlas and Delta families as the only launch vehicles that can reach the full range of orbits and carry our heaviest payloads.

United Launch Alliance builds and flies the Atlas and Delta families for the U.S. Government and commercial customers, and they currently enjoy an unprecedented record of successful launches, 90 of which were accomplished under the EELV program. This exceptional achievement was accomplished with very high levels of mission assurance, including rigorous engineering review and component testing.

In this constrained budget environment, we believe that competition between certified launch providers on a level playing field is the best mechanism to incentivize the innovation required to do so. The simple fact is that the Delta family is not cost competitive, and with the restrictions on the use of Atlas, the Department must continue to look for alternative launch capabilities which are compliant with the law.

STATUTORY CHALLENGES

Section 1604 of the 2015 NDAA requires that we develop a domestic next-generation rocket propulsion system suitable for national security use by 2019, that it be available for purchase by all domestic space launch providers, be developed using full and open competition, and that we examine the benefits of public-private partnerships to do so. We have examined the feasibility of public-private partnerships through the use of a Request for Information (RFI). The Air Force released a RFI in August 2014 to solicit industry inputs on propulsion and launch systems. The conclusion from the RFI responses is that a solution at the propulsion level alone would not result in a launch vehicle solution capable of meeting the National Security Space (NSS) requirements. In contrast to the early days of space exploration, the U.S. Government no longer controls the technical baseline through ownership of the designs or integrating the launch systems. Shared investment with launch providers and competition for launch services—much like the original EELV program and the NASA Commercial Orbital Transportation Services (COTS), Cargo, and Commercial Crew programs—is the most cost-effective approach to transition from the RD–180, while ensuring the existence of two or more domestic, commercially viable launch providers that also meet NSS requirements by the end of fiscal year 2022.

The Defense Appropriations for fiscal year 2015 provided $220,000,000 to accelerate rocket propulsion system development to fiscal year 2019. The agreement directs the Department, in consultation with the NASA Administrator, to develop an affordable, innovative, and competitive strategy for this development effort that includes an assessment of the potential benefits and challenges of using public-private partnerships, innovative teaming arrangements, and small business considerations. The strategy should include plans for targeted risk reduction projects and technology maturation efforts to buy down risk and accelerate potential launch system solutions.

Section 1608 of the 2015 National Defense Authorization Act (NDAA) restricts the use of the RD–180 rocket engine. Just as the Department complied with Congressional direction to incentivize industry to adopt the RD–180 in the 1990s, we are now taking steps to eliminate strategic reliance on Russian engines while maintaining assured access to space. As we testified last year, we continue to believe that provision of 18 RD–180 engines will be sufficient to maintain a competitive environment during the transition period. The Department is committed to transitioning off of the RD–180 as quickly as possible while minimizing impacts to national security

LAUNCH SERVICES, NOT ROCKET ENGINES

Assured access to space requires end-to-end space launch services and not just a rocket engine. As many Department of Defense witnesses have testified to this and other congressional committees, simply replacing the RD–180 with a new engine will not deliver the performance of the current design. To explain why, it is necessary to describe the relationship between a rocket and its engine, as well as how modern rockets are different from earlier launch systems.

To deliver a payload to orbit safely, rocket engines must release and direct tremendous amounts of energy in order to escape gravity, while protecting the payload from the shock and vibration unleashed by that energy. In the early days of space launch, the Government owned the technical baseline, and built larger engines and heavier structures in the rocket body to handle the shock. However, this approach resulted in launch systems that were both inefficient and very expensive. Modern launch systems are designed to be more efficient, by reducing the weight of the rocket structure itself. To handle the stresses, every modern rocket is designed around its engine and the performance envelope defined by its payloads. For example, the Atlas V was built around the RD–180 engine to efficiently deliver a wide range of payloads into a variety of orbits. As a result, any effort to simply replace the RD–

180 with a substitute engine would require extensive design and engineering changes, as well as significant dynamic and acoustic testing, and would ultimately result in a new launch system, which would require recertification.

UNITED LAUNCH ALLIANCE AND EELV LAUNCH CAPABILITY

Consistent with the Commercial Space Act, the Department procures launch services rather than the individual hardware components used to provide those services. The Department does not have contractual control over ULA's internal allocation of RD–180 engines; therefore, ULA is in the best position to provide detailed information relating to the timing of ULA's assignment of the five RD–180 engines that meet the requirements of the Fiscal Year 2015 NDAA without the need for a waiver. We understand that ULA seeks to minimize the inventory it carries and the time between engine testing and launch. Given this understanding along with the engine production timelines and launch manifest, both the Department and NASA do not believe ULA's decision to assign these five engines to support its current manifest was early to need.

The current EELV Launch Capability (ELC) arrangement is a contract option awarded as part of the EELV contract in 2006 to fund the fixed cost of maintaining ULA launch infrastructure critical to assuring access to space. The purpose of ELC was to ensure that ULA, as the sole launch provider at the time, could be ready to launch when critical national security payloads were needed, as opposed to waiting for a slot on a manifest. It accomplished this goal by stabilizing the engineering workforce, supporting launch infrastructure maintenance, funding costs associated with the Government's independent mission assurance process, and sustaining launch site operations. This approach was appropriate for the EELV sole-source environment, and resulted in both cost savings and increased flexibility for the Government in scheduling launches. As we transition to a competitive environment, the Department has reached an agreement with ULA on the equitable allocation of ELC cost to each launch for the remainder of the contract duration, in order to ensure a level playing field for competing launch providers. The current ELC structure will end with the completion of the EELV Phase I Block Buy contract, currently projected in fiscal year 2019.

WAY AHEAD

The Department delivered a strategy to the Congress in August 2015 that described our use of targeted risk reduction projects and technology maturation efforts to buy down risk and accelerate potential launch system solutions. Our objective is a more commercial model than the Department would normally follow. We intend to competitively select future launch service providers and to enter into tailored public-private partnership business arrangements that result in affordable, competitive launch services for national security missions. The exact form of these arrangements will depend on the needs of each of the selected launch service providers. The strategy also calls for the use of Other Transaction Authority (OTA) agreements, consistent with the Fiscal Year 2016 NDAA, which broadens the use of OTAs. We plan to execute innovative teaming arrangements and joint investments with industry partners for launch system development (which is expected to include propulsion system development) consistent with the launch service provider's business needs and our launch services needs.

Unfortunately, at this time we are constrained by statute to work only on space propulsion engines. The Department would strongly prefer to not have to pay for the development of an RD–180 engine replacement that would benefit only one launch service provider. Consistent with this legal constraint, we are currently implementing robust risk reduction and technology maturation efforts covering propulsion system Material and Manufacturing Development, Advanced Technologies, Modeling & Design Tools, and Critical Component integration and testing through the use of Broad Agency Announcement awards, which involve universities, NASA, and the Air Force Research Laboratory. We expect some of this work will transition into the launch service provider public-private partnership agreements we intend to award in fiscal year 2017.

In order to transition from the RD–180 and ensure the Department has at least two viable domestic launch service providers for assured access to space as quickly as possible, we must shift from propulsion development to launch capability development as soon as possible. The Department would greatly appreciate the committee's support for our planned launch service acquisition activities.

CONCLUSION

Mister Chairman, Mr. Ranking Member, Members of the Committee, the Department is committed to transitioning off the Russian RD–180 rocket engine. We must maintain assured access to space, and we believe a public-private partnership with launch providers is the best means to that end. Maintaining at least two of the existing systems until at least two launch providers are available will be necessary to protect our Nation's assured access to space. As we move forward, we respectfully request this committee allow the Department the flexibility to develop and acquire the launch capabilities our warfighters and Intelligence Community need. Thank you for your support.

STATEMENT OF HONORABLE FRANK KENDALL III, UNDER SECRETARY OF DEFENSE FOR ACQUISITION, TECHNOLOGY AND LOGISTICS

Mr. KENDALL. Thank you, Mr. Chairman.

Chairman McCain, Ranking Member Reed, members of the committee, I am pleased to be here with Secretary James today to answer your questions about the Department of Defense's space launch program. Secretary James has already provided you with an overview of our priorities, some background, and our plans. I would like to use my opening statement to say more about the acquisition approach we would like to use to meet the Department's priorities of assured access to space, meaning at least two affordable and reliable sources of launch services for national security system launches, competition using commercial launch service providers to control cost, and ending the use of the RD–180 Russian engine for Department of Defense launches.

The first thing I would like to emphasize is that the Department does not buy rockets or engines. We do not buy launch systems or propulsion systems. What we do buy is the transportation of our satellites to space by launch service providers. Given our desire to eliminate usage of the Russian RD–180 engine, which is currently used on ULA's Atlas launch system when ULA provides launch services to the Department, the obvious and direct thing for the Department to do would seem to be pay for a new engine to replace the RD–180. There are three problems with this.

First, engines and rockets are designed to work together. A copy of the RD–180 would be an Atlas engine, and it would not be of general use to the commercial launch service community. We would likely be helping one specific commercial launch service provider, as Secretary James said, with one specific launch system, the venerable Atlas.

Second, this would be expensive. Current estimates are that this would take about $3 billion.

Third, the Department does not need an engine, certainly not an Atlas engine. It does need assured access to space through reliable, affordable, and efficient launch service providers.

Second is the context in which we expect to acquire launch services over the next decade or longer. The commercial space launch business and space as an operational domain are both in transition. A number of commercial enterprises are planning large-scale constellations involving hundreds or even thousands of satellites. In this environment, the Department should be able to take advantage of the economies of scale associated with a large number of commercial launches each year. This potential market is motivating launch service companies like SpaceX, ULA, and others to invest in more modern and efficient space launch systems. The Department does not need to and should not carry all the cost of developing more efficient space launch systems. We need to capitalize on these commercial investments.

Let me provide a word of caution, however. Some of us have seen this movie before. In the early 1990s, it was the promise of constellations like Teledesic, Iridium, and Global Star that led the Department to believe future launch costs would be much less than they turned out to be. We cannot be sure what will happen this time. We do know that significant investments are being made in the planned commercial constellations, and we should do our best to take advantage of the opportunity that this environment presents.

From an operational perspective, Mr. Chairman, as you indicated, the Department is concerned about the ongoing foreign military acquisition of anti-satellite systems by countries like Russia and China. This development is causing a major rethinking of our space system designs with resiliency to possible attack now a much more important operational and technical consideration.

One approach that offers some promise is called disaggregation, with the replacement of current small numbers of highly capable satellites with large numbers of satellites that are more distributed capabilities. This development also suggests the need for more efficient launch service providers to field those constellations.

Given that we need launch services and not launch systems and given that we think the future commercial and military environments are both moving us toward the opportunity and the need for more efficient launch service providers, the answers seem clear. The Department has the opportunity to enter business arrangements with prospective launch service providers using a commercial model. The basic business deal we have in mind is that the Department will, through competition, provide at least two launch service providers with some of the capital they need to develop, test, and certify the launch systems they will use to provide us with launch services in the future, including any unique DOD requirements. In return for this investment, the Department will acquire the right to purchase launch services in the future at competitive prices and some degree of assurance that those systems will actually be available.

This commercial model is an innovative, out-of-the-box approach being taken by the Department. We sometimes refer to it as a public-private partnership. The exact form of these business arrangements will take will be very dependent on the unique needs of each competing prospective launch service provider. The Department has received industry responses to formal requests for information that Secretary James commented on which tell us that this concept has a real chance of success.

Our next step will be to release a draft request for proposals in the next few months. Contingent on the responses to the draft, we hope to have final RFPs on the street by the end of the year to support awards in fiscal year 2017.

In most acquisition strategies, the Department specifies the product or service that it desires and industry bids to provide the specified deliverables. In this case, industry will have an important role in defining the terms of the arrangement or contract. Each selected launch service provider is expected to offer unique terms that will have to be negotiated.

The competition will be conducted on a "best value" basis. The best value determination will take a number of factors into account. These plans are not complete, but the factors are likely to include the technical risk of completing the launch system and achieving certification, the schedule to provide launch services without Russian engines, the soundness of the business case to provide commercial launch services efficiently, the cost of any "not to exceed" future launch service options for DOD, and of course, the amount and timing of DOD funding needed to complete development and certification of the proposed launch system.

Secretary James and I would like to ask the committee for its support in pursuing this novel commercial model. We believe it is very consistent with the direction to use more commercial acquisition models that the committee provided in the Fiscal Year 2016 NDAA. We are anxious to move forward so that we can end the use of the RD–180 and take advantage of the emerging commercial space launch service market. We will need your support for this approach in the 2017 NDAA by removing, as Secretary James said, the existing constraints that restrict our use of funds to only propulsion systems.

We would be happy to answer any questions that you may have.

Chairman McCAIN. Well, thank you very much.

Mr. Secretary, I certainly appreciate your and Secretary James? advocacy for competition here.

How much money are we paying, up until we prohibited it, to ULA just for staying in business? I guess it is called sustainable. Is that not about $800 million a year?

Ms. JAMES. That is about right.

Chairman McCAIN. So we have been paying since—what—2006 ULA $800 million a year to stay in business. It is kind of hard to compete if you are in the private sector when the Federal Government—for doing nothing, when the Department of Defense pays you $800 million a year for a, quote, sustainable. Then when it comes to the launch, a GPS III launch competition, they do not compete. Is that not a violation of the $800 million a year that we are paying them?

Mr. KENDALL. Senator McCain, let me address what we——

Chairman McCAIN. Just tell me. Just answer the question. Should they be paid $800 million a year to be, quote, sustainable and they do not even compete on a launch? I would like an answer to the question. Should they have been paid $800 million a year?

Mr. KENDALL. We agree with you that they should be bidding on our launches, and we are most disappointed——

Chairman McCAIN. I am asking the question, should they be paid $800 million a year for sustainable and not even bid on a launch? That is a pretty straightforward question, Mr. Secretary.

Mr. KENDALL. Senator, we are all upset that they did not bid on the proposal——

Chairman McCAIN. What is the penalty? What is the penalty for that?

Mr. KENDALL. As Secretary James indicated, we are looking into penalties.

Chairman MCCAIN. Well, you are looking into it. I see. Since 2006—that is 9 years, $800 million a year—that is astronomical, that sum of money of taxpayers? dollars, and after paying them $800 million a year for—my calculation—9 or 10 years, then they do not even compete on a launch. Is that the appropriate use of the taxpayers? dollars?

Ms. JAMES. Senator, if I could jump in. You heard me in my opening statement say what worked in a sole-source environment will be anachronistic once we get off of the block buy and get beyond it.

Chairman MCCAIN. How can you compete when your competition is being paid $800 million a year just to stay in business?

Mr. KENDALL. Senator McCain, the ELC contract covers fixed and some variable costs associated with ULA's launch infrastructure. It was put in place to cover those costs to provide some stability.

Chairman MCCAIN. Do you know of any other arrangement that we have with any defense contractor that pays them for doing nothing?

Mr. KENDALL. Senator McCain, I cannot think of one off the top of my head.

Chairman MCCAIN. Except staying in business?

Mr. KENDALL. I would like to explain how——

Chairman MCCAIN. Do you know of any other? I would like you to answer the questions. Do you know of any other Federal arrangement with any other defense corporation where you pay them $800 million a year simply to remain in business? Do you know of another contract of that nature?

Mr. KENDALL. I am not aware of another one similar to this.

Chairman MCCAIN. Thank you.

I am sure you are probably not familiar with the names Igor Komarov or Sergey Chemezov or maybe even Dmitry Rogozin. Those all are three individuals that the United States has sanctioned, and all three of those have something in common. They are on the board of directors of the organization that we are now buying these rocket engines from. A Reuters? investigation showed that the Russian rocket engine manufacturer, Energomosh, and Pratt & Whitney Rocketdyne collects $93 million in cost markups. The article uncovers that in the past RD–Amross was investigated by the Defense Contract Management Agency which determined that in a previous contract that RD–Amross had collected $80 million in, quote, unallowable excessive pass-through charges. So we now have senior Russian politicians, friends of Vladimir Putin, in the management that are making tens of millions of dollars in the pass-through money that is paid for the Russian rocket engines.

Does that disturb you, Madam Secretary?

Ms. JAMES. Yes.

Chairman MCCAIN. You did not know anything about it?

Ms. JAMES. You brought to my attention several of those names yesterday, and you heard the action I took as follow-up yesterday, Senator.

Chairman MCCAIN. You were never made aware of all this information before I brought it to your attention, even though it was public knowledge as far back as 2014?

Ms. JAMES. The Russian names you gave me yesterday——

Chairman MCCAIN. No. I am talking about the $93 million in markups that are just pass-through money.

Ms. JAMES. What I am aware of is the Reuters article. I am also aware——

Chairman MCCAIN. Were you aware of it? Were you aware of it?

Ms. JAMES. Prior to the Reuters article?

Chairman MCCAIN. The article was in 2014. Did you know about it in 2014?

Ms. JAMES. I read the article in 2014.

Chairman MCCAIN. Then what action did you take?

Ms. JAMES. I inquired about it and learned that in the year 2011 there was a price reasonableness analysis done between Air Force and DCMA, which is the regulating authority——

Chairman MCCAIN. That is 2011. In 2014, the Defense Contract Management Agency determined that in a previous contract they had collected $80 million in unallowable excessive pass-through charges. Were you aware of that, the Defense Contract Management Agency determination?

Ms. JAMES. My understanding is that was fixed for this contract of the block buy.

Chairman MCCAIN. It was fixed?

Ms. JAMES. That is my understanding.

Chairman MCCAIN. In other words, none of these individuals are now making money off of the sale of——

Ms. JAMES. The block buy was price reasonable per the analysis is my understanding.

Chairman MCCAIN. Mr. Rogozin and Chemezov and Komarov are not making any money off of this?

Ms. JAMES. I cannot talk to that. I have asked the appropriate authorities——

Chairman MCCAIN. You should be able to talk to it. These people are people who have been sanctioned by the United States of America.

Ms. JAMES. I am sure the appropriate authorities will get to the bottom of it.

Chairman MCCAIN. We are giving them millions of dollars of American tax dollars.

Well, my time has expired but this is really, really, really remarkable, and we intend, frankly, to, in a totally bipartisan basis, try to fix this problem. When some of us are surprised, when our taxpayers are angry, when the people who think that we are not working for them in Washington and see this kind of thing where we are paying a company $800 million a year just to stay in business and then they do not even bid on a launch, you express concern when we are giving tens of millions of dollars to Russian corrupt oligarchs and taking no action to really resolve it and then, of course, work behind our backs, the authorizing committee, to try to nullify the action taken by this committee after hearings, after votes, after a debate, after talking about it on the floor of the Senate and you support the undermining of what we tried to do. Unacceptable.

Senator Reed?

Senator REED. Thank you very much, Mr. Chairman.

Secretary James and Secretary Kendall, could you give your opinion on whether we could be in a situation by 2018 where we only have one launch provider? What circumstances could lead to this? Because that would be a vulnerability that would be significant. Madam Secretary or Mr. Secretary?

Mr. KENDALL. We have been concerned for some time that with the course that we are on, we may end up with one launch service provider. ULA has been competing, has done one competition with SpaceX. ULA is disadvantaged in that they have an older system and the costs associated with that system. They have to bid the systems that they have. SpaceX has a more modern system that they are providing.

We do make adjustments and we have corrected for a shortfall in the ELC contract that Senator McCain asked about so that we have a fair playing field. Secretary James mentioned this in her opening testimony. So we are making adjustments that further disadvantage ULA because they will now essentially be paying a penalty for the fact that the contract that Senator McCain was talking about exists and some of their costs are covered by that contract.

So we are concerned that going forward they will not be very competitive. They recognize that and they know they need to get to a more efficient and affordable launch system, and they are trying to get on that path. Their viability and their ability to do that depends upon them having continued business over the next few years. That business comes in the form of Atlas and Delta launches. The Department stops using 180s, and it is questionable as to whether or not ULA will be able to remain in business using only Deltas.

We will not use Deltas as a preferred system because it is much more expensive than Atlas and it is much more expensive than SpaceX's system. So SpaceX would be the default almost automatically. They would be in an almost sole-source position at that point. It is questionable whether or not ULA would survive. So we could very well be in a situation with only one launch service provider.

ULA has provided us with 80 or 90 successful launches in a row. So that is a very important national capability. We have been able to rely on them very successfully. So we are not comfortable with being left with the risk of only being dependent upon SpaceX.

Senator REED. Madam Secretary, your comments?

Ms. JAMES. I really do not have anything to add. I think that was a good assessment.

Senator REED. Secretary Kendall, just to reiterate, the point I think you made is that your conclusion is that we cannot rely just on a ULA Delta lift system and SpaceX. So the Atlas will be needed. Is that your conclusion? What underlies that conclusion?

Mr. KENDALL. Delta is a possibility as a second source. The problem is it is much more expensive than Atlas or the SpaceX's Falcon 9. It also has some issues in terms of production capacity. There would be a multiyear lead time to get Delta up to the rate that we would need to replace the Atlas launches. There are some differences in terms of preparation time and so on that are not as significant. So Delta does not look to us like a good alternative to Atlas as a second source.

The intelligence community has asked that we look into that.

Senator REED. Delta and the SpaceX would be using non-Russian engines.

Mr. KENDALL. That would be all non-Russian engines. That is right.

The intelligence community uses mostly Delta launches. So they have been interested in doing more Deltas because that would lower their cost for their launches because of the economies associated with that. For the Department of Defense, that does not look like the best business thing for us by a wide margin.

As Secretary James mentioned, we will take another look at this. We will take a deep look at it again. I will be surprised if the answer comes out differently.

Senator REED. The chairman has outline some very disturbing aspects of this program going back many, many years, and we cannot deny that. In fact, his efforts particularly have been trying to fix this program.

What I think you have suggested is the best path to a non-subsidized, competitive marketplace is this public-private partnership approach which you are talking about so that we will no longer have to put someone on retainer who may or may not participate given their bottom line decisions. Is that sort of an overall sense of where you would like to go?

Mr. KENDALL. That is correct.

Senator Reed, if I could take a moment to talk about the ELC contract, I would like to explain what that contract actually does, if I could do that.

Senator REED. Yes. My time is limited, but within a minute if you can do that.

Mr. KENDALL. It pays for costs associated with ULA's infrastructure, and it pays some variable costs associated with the launches. It was set up to provide a stable base for ULA to plan on and to have in place the capability to support about eight launches a year. When we had only ULA as a source of launches, that was a very reasonable business thing to do. It allowed us to take some of the variation and uncertainty out of the market and to stabilize this. We have been successful with the ELC in bringing some of those costs down. Nothing was as successful as the block buy and the introduction of competition. So that has been a very good motivator and we want to continue that.

The ELC business deal was not a bad business deal. It is not a bad contract. It is not a subsidy. The original contract included a provision for ULA obtaining commercial launches outside the Department of Defense. If it did so, we made an adjustment in the contract so that there would be no subsidy for those commercial launches. What we did not put in the original contract was a similar provision for DOD competitions because at the time we started out, we did not anticipate competitions. We only had ULA to buy launches from.

Now that SpaceX is competing, we realize had a problem there. SpaceX called that to our attention. They were correct.

So we have gone back and we have negotiated an agreement that changes the ELC contract so that there is no unfair advantage to ULA in a competition with SpaceX or another competitor for DOD launches. We have made a significant adjustment, and I mentioned it earlier. It further raises the effective cost of ULA's bids making them less competitive, which adds to our concern about their viability.

Senator REED. Thank you. Thank you, Mr. Chairman. Thank you, Madam Secretary.

Chairman MCCAIN. There are other competitors besides SpaceX, Blue Origin, and a number of others. So to somehow portray it as just between those two is, of course, totally inaccurate.

Senator Sessions?

Senator SESSIONS. Thank you.

Mr. Kendall, with regard to that point that Senator McCain made, are there other competitors, and what is the status of their ability to compete?

Mr. KENDALL. There are people who would like to be competitors, but they are not competitors yet. Blue Origin that Senator McCain mentioned is in development. The launch system providers all have modern systems in development to some degree. Orbital ATK is also considering a new system.

So what we would like to do through the public-private partnerships that I mentioned is get business deals with at least two of these potential future suppliers so that we have modern systems after we get off of the RD–180 to replace it. Right now, the only certified launch providers are SpaceX and ULA.

Senator SESSIONS. Well, first, this committee has been unanimous and I have been firmly committed to getting off the RD–180 as soon as possible. I will acknowledge that I have been critical of the length of time, but as I have learned more about it, I realize you have a more complicated situation than most of us fully understand.

So in the interim, you have asked the committee last year for 14 RD–180s to be provided, and the committee, after much discussion in the subcommittee, was acceptable to your number. We ended up with nine. Senator McCain suggested nine, and that is the decision of our committee. Then the Appropriations Committee basically said to the Defense Department we will not put a cap on it. You decide how many RD–180s will be purchased. So that has caused a disturbance, let us say.

Secretary James, you mentioned 18 now. You think it may be more than 14. Why do you need 18? Is this some sort of interim supply while this bid process goes forward? What is the reason you might need more than 14?

Ms. JAMES. If I may clarify, Senator. If you remember, there were five engines originally available, if you recall. Last year what we said was we said a total—this included the five—of about 18. You are saying 19. My recollection it was 18.

Senator SESSIONS. 18.

Ms. JAMES. On the order of about 18 to us seemed reasonable to get us over the hump and allow for competition as we transitioned to a full-up competitive environment away from the Russian-built engine. So 18 seemed to be a reasonable number to deal with to get over that hump. There were 34 competitions during this interim period, and to have 18 engines against 34 competitions seemed to us to be reasonable. So I was simply restating that that was and remains our position, a prudent, reasonable way forward. That is what I was meaning to say.

Senator SESSIONS. Now, the committee, as has been noted, authorized $220 million. You referred to that, and there is some more money left over from previous appropriations to fund this transition. What is taking so long, and what can Congress do? You have suggested there are some problems with the mandates we have placed on you. What are those problems? So do we have enough money? Are we on track to have more than one competitor?

You would expect, Mr. Kendall, that any competition would be cheaper than the RD–180 ULA current system? If they are not cheaper, they are not going to win the proposal. Is that right? Where are we in this process and what is going to happen?

Mr. KENDALL. I would agree with that last statement, Senator Sessions.

Senator SESSIONS. The last statement was that transitioning from the ULA system to the new system that SpaceX is competing for and others could compete for you would expect a cheaper launch system.

Mr. KENDALL. I expect a modernized system by any competitor to be cheaper, and it would not make any sense for us to——

Senator SESSIONS. It would be fully American.

Mr. KENDALL. Yes, absolutely.

The problem we have right now is that the current NDAA restricts us to work on propulsion systems, rocket engines. As I mentioned in my statement and Secretary James mentioned, that is not what we need. We need launch service providers with full launch systems that can take us into space. We want to get business deals that get us to that goal and that give us some assurance of reasonable prices for future launches. So that is where we need to go, and we need the constraint that we currently have removed so that we can do that effectively and efficiently.

We have been trying to comply with the law, and we have complied with the law throughout this. We have tried to find a way to move forward by investing in propulsion systems. That is what the contracts that Secretary James talked about do for us. They are propulsion systems and we think they are linked to possible future launch systems, but what we really want is the commitment to get us that full future capability and we cannot do that with the constraint that we have right now.

Senator SESSIONS. Have you submitted a proposed legislative change that we can consider?

Mr. KENDALL. I do not think we have, but we would be happy to do that.

Senator SESSIONS. The reasons why would be appropriate I think. Thank you.

Mr. KENDALL. Yes, sir.

Chairman MCCAIN. Let me just point out that it is not rocket engine. It is rocket engines that we are buying from the Russians, not anything else. That is why we are focusing our attention on Russians making hundreds of millions of dollars. So we are not restricting anything except that we want to get rid of our dependency on Russian rocket engines. So for you to keep saying that we are making restrictions on it, we are not. We are not restricting SpaceX. We are not restricting Blue Origin. We are not restricting anybody that wants to get into the game. What we want to do is get out of the Russian rocket engine business and stop subsidizing one military industrial complex for $800 million a year of the taxpayers? money for nothing, and then they turn around and refuse to bid after we have given them $800 million to stay in business.

Senator Heinrich?

Senator HEINRICH. Secretary James and Under Secretary Kendall, welcome.

I remain supportive of efforts to end our Nation's reliance on the Russian-built RD–180 rocket engine, recognizing, as you said, that we need a complete launch capability.

Since the 2014 Russian invasion of Crimea, I have certainly supported our Nation's ongoing investment to develop a new engine to replace that RD–180 as important to accomplish that goal. Over the last 3 years, we have appropriated $403 million I believe to accomplish that goal. Congress has been pretty clear and bipartisan in its desire to pursue a replacement engine and to do that quickly.

I think what you are hearing here is a frustration in the speed at which we have been able to accomplish that and what appears from the outside as well as sort of a salami slice approach to all of this.

So I want to ask what work specifically is being done in these other contracts. Is this work specifically tied to developing a replacement engine for the RD–180, or are other efforts being funded with this money that will not necessarily get us to that launch capability?

Ms. JAMES. I will start and then maybe Mr. Kendall can jump in.

The $400 million and some that you referenced, Senator, includes $227 million I believe, if memory serves me, which was the fiscal year 2016 authorization/appropriation, which has been available to us for roughly 5 to 6 weeks. It only just became law in December. So the figures that I gave you were our efforts to obligate as quickly as possible the 2014 and 2015 money. As I was attempting to portray, the vast majority of that now has been obligated, and we expect the balance to be obligated quite soon pending successful negotiations with industry. I do want to underscore that. It takes two to tango, and we can have all the urgency in the world, but we cannot give away the farm if the negotiation does not go well because the farm belongs to the U.S. taxpayers. So we are trying to have that balance between speed but getting a good deal for the taxpayer.

You mentioned spreading the money around or salami slicing, words to that effect. The first part of this plan that I laid out for you has to do with what we call technology maturation and risk reduction. This is a typical approach when you are dealing with something new and difficult. Believe me, this is hard science. I have talked to enough of the technologists to believe that this is not as easy as it sounds. For something that difficult, something where the U.S. Government has not invested hugely in the past few decades, it is a prudent approach to try to reduce the risk and then share those learnings across industry so that it helps others in the future. So that is why this money is being sent to different locations in a full and open way, by the way, because I do want to emphasize that.

Senator HEINRICH. I recognize that. Are you worried that by sort of spreading this across multiple pathways that you actually push back the timeline to ending our reliance on this core capability, which is the RD–180?

Mr. KENDALL. I think the confusion is about what we are trying to do and how we are trying to do it and how the contracts we have let get us down that path.

As I mentioned in my opening comments, one of the paths we could have taken was to simply buy an RD–180 replacement, buy a look-alike clone, if you will, of the RD–180. If we had done that or if we did do that, we would be buying ULA a new engine for Atlas, which would be perfectly fine for ULA, but it would not get us off of Atlas. It would not get us a modern, efficient, affordable launch system as a viable competitor to others like SpaceX.

So what we did, given the restriction in the law—and the restriction came from the House side of the House Armed Services Committee in their bill. It basically said we cannot use the funds we are appropriated to develop or procure a new launch vehicle or related infrastructure. We were restricted to development of propulsion systems.

So what we have done is look at the propulsion systems and evaluate them for ones that have a reasonable chance of being in a future launch system. Propulsion is not just about the first stage, which is what the RD–180 is. It is about the upper stages and other things.

Senator HEINRICH. I understand.

Mr. KENDALL. So the two contracts we have awarded—one of them is for some upper stage work; the other is for solid rocket motor work. We are going to award two more, which will cover— I cannot talk about the details of those yet because they are not awarded.

So each of these is intended to move us down the path and reduce some of the technical risk associated with getting a new launch system that is much more efficient and affordable and modern. It does not accomplish that goal by itself. It is a step in the right direction.

We would like to move much more quickly and directly to the goal that we have in mind. That is where we are asking the committee's support to allow us to do.

Senator HEINRICH. Thank you both. Obviously, my time has expired.

I hope at some point you can get to the heart as well of dealing with whether the sustainment as a contract exercise is paying ULA to effectively do nothing. My time has expired and I will give back my time, Chairman.

Chairman MCCAIN. Senator Cotton?

Senator COTTON. Secretary James, do you believe that Russia is an enemy of the United States?

Ms. JAMES. I have said publicly before and I will say again, sir, that I think Russia is the top threat to the United States.

Senator COTTON. So you agree with the testimony of General Dunford and several other members of the Joint Chiefs that Russia is our number one threat geopolitically in the world?

Ms. JAMES. Yes.

Senator COTTON. Has the United States ever had assured access to space?

Ms. JAMES. That is our top job is to make sure we have assured access to space.

Senator COTTON. Under the current understanding, have we had assured access to space?

Ms. JAMES. Yes.

Senator COTTON. We have. Okay.

Could we end our reliance on these Russian-made rockets today and still maintain assured access to space by relying on Falcon 9 and Delta IV?

Ms. JAMES. I would say it is theoretically possible, but the devil would be very much in the details.

Senator COTTON. So both of those rockets are certified. They can carry all kinds of lift, heavy, intermediate, and so forth. Why is that only theoretically possible?

Ms. JAMES. There is a current manifest based on warfighter needs and the intelligence community needs, and that manifest, to a certain degree, depends on a mixture of engines. If you were to suddenly swing and take one type of engine away and say hereforth it must be only this sort of engine, that would require probably delays in launches. I am thinking certainly it would be a lot more money because Delta is a much more expensive proposition. It would have to be reworked. There would be a lot of details to work through.

Senator COTTON. What kind of gap would you fear if that were the case?

Ms. JAMES. Without doing an analysis, detailed, I would be totally guessing. I would guess years, but that is a guess.

Senator COTTON. What is the current status of the possibility of replacing the RD–180 with an American-made rocket engine, say the AR–1 or the BE–4?

Ms. JAMES. We are marching toward 2019. That is the way all of our urgency is directed. Industry tells us and we certainly think it is possible, though it is going to be challenging to make 2019 for an engine. I must say an engine alone will not get us to space. It needs to be integrated with a rocket. It needs to be tested. It needs to be certified. To get all of that done, to have a launch capability, will be longer than 2019.

Senator COTTON. Which theoretically we could do now though with the Falcon 9 and the Delta IV, since they are certified.

Ms. JAMES. I say theoretically but it would require looking into all of those details.

Senator COTTON. I am struggling with why you cannot maintain the promise of future competition if you just pursue a split buy for a few years of the 9 and the IV until this new engine is developed, if it is a top priority not to rely on these Russian-made rocket engines. Secretary Kendall, you look like you want to——

Mr. KENDALL. There are several problems with that. One is, obviously, the cost of Delta. It is tens of millions of dollars more than Atlas or Falcon 9.

Senator COTTON. We have paid $800 million for no activity.

Mr. KENDALL. We paid $800 million toward specific costs associated with getting the infrastructure that ULA has for launching both Atlas and Delta. That cost is associated with the capacity to launch eight launches per year. Those costs have been reviewed many times. They are reasonable costs for us to bear. It is not nothing, as the chairman indicated. I am sorry about that.

The difficulties with Delta are its effect—the loss of Atlas? effect on ULA's viability; the cost of Delta, tens of millions of dollars more; the amount of time it would take us to ramp up production of Delta, which would be on the order of 3 years; and then some other minor issues that we could probably work our way around if we had to. So it is not impossible. It is just very difficult.

Ms. JAMES. Could I also add? Delta is the one that is not commercially competitive. So if we were to swing in that direction, we would be the sole customer I believe. The price—again, likely, but we would have to examine the details—would go up even more than the differential today between Delta and Atlas because this ELC arrangement you have been hearing so much about—those costs I can pretty well guarantee you would somehow be calculated into the new price of Delta. Whether you call it an ELC arrangement or whether you call it something different, I believe the U.S. taxpayer would bear those costs.

Senator COTTON. My time is concluding. I will say that in a program that spends billions of dollars over the years, tens of millions of dollars of costs to develop an American-made capability so we are not depending on our number geopolitical adversary's industrial base seems to me a reasonable cost to bear, in particular when their industrial base is going to be able to use those profits in part to develop their counter-space capabilities. We are going to be putting into our rockets parts that are made in Russia that for all we know might be corrupted or have some kind of cyber threat to them. So I would opine that we might want to consider bearing those costs to develop domestic capabilities as quickly as we can to include the two rockets that are currently certified.

Chairman MCCAIN. Senator Hirono?

Senator HIRONO. Thank you, Mr. Chairman.

I believe this committee has made clear that we do not want to continue to rely on these Russian-made engines.

Secretary James, I am interested in the portion of your testimony wherein you say—and both of you have testified to this—at this time you are constrained by statute to work only on space propulsion engines. So I know that one of my colleagues had already asked this question, Senator Sessions. I would really like to see where in the NDAA you find this constraining language. First I would like to have that identified, and then I would like a proposal. We would like to see a proposal for additional language so that we can assure ourselves the access to space that is our goal. You may not have that language right now, but I certainly would be interested in those two areas that I asked about.

Mr. KENDALL. Senator, if I may. The section is section 1606 of the fiscal year 2016 NDAA. We do not have language for you today, but we would be happy to provide that.

Senator HIRONO. The reason I am pursuing this is because there seems to be a dispute as to whether or not we do have constraining language on the Department.

I would like to turn to small satellites and operationally responsive space (ORS). I am a supporter of the ORS office, especially in the area of developing smaller, cheaper systems, which can be launched more fast than conventional systems. I know that our more complex and larger systems will be needed for many payloads, but where the smaller and less complex systems can be used, we should do so.

I know that you are investing in this. This is for Secretary James. I also believe strongly in research and development for these systems. Can you share your thoughts on ORS and what you would like to see in the future and talk about the R&D [research & development] side and the involvement of industry, universities, and labs as we develop these faster, smaller, and cheaper launch systems?

Ms. JAMES. So, Senator, I am a believer in ORS as well. I mean, there was a period where this was not being funded, and we are funding this going forward. So I certainly am a believer. When it comes to small satellites, this is of great interest to the Department. It is a trend, I will say, in the commercial arena. You have talked about universities and industry. We are in constant discussions with those who are attempting to excel so that we can learn from them and partner wherever possible.

The other thing I will say about small satellites is it does hold promise for us in certain arenas for greater resiliency. So it is like you do not put all your eggs in one basket. You spread it out, so to speak. So it could help us in our resiliency quest, and also they tend to be a whole lot less expensive. So for all of these reasons, it is of great interest.

Now, with all that said, we have to make sure that when we launch something, that it is going to fit within our architecture and that we do some proper technology demonstrations and experiments in advance. Indeed, this is where ORS can come into play in a bigger way.

You may recall ORS is working on a couple of things right now. They are working on a follow-on for the SBSS, space-based space surveillance, program. They are also doing technology demonstration—or they are about to—with respect to the weather.

So a big believer in ORS and very interested in small satellites to help us in the future.

Senator HIRONO. Secretary Kendall, would you like to add anything to that?

Mr. KENDALL. No. I think Secretary James covered it very well.

One comment I would make is that as we move into an era where desegregated constellations are possible and we would be living in an environment in space with some massive commercial constellations in low earth orbit, that as we deal with the threats that Senator McCain mentioned, the attractiveness of an ORS type of an approach becomes much more so.

Senator HIRONO. Are we putting enough resources into this part of our access to space goal in terms of money for R&D?

Ms. JAMES. I believe we have it about right.

Senator HIRONO. What is it?

Ms. JAMES. Well, the details, of course, we will roll out shortly as part of our fiscal year 2017 budget and the accompanying 5-year plan. You will see that we have funded ORS throughout.

Senator HIRONO. I am going to have continuing interest in that, especially as I also serve on the Intelligence Committee.

Secretary Kendall, there has been a discussion within Congress on the idea of giving more responsibility in the acquisition process to the Service Chiefs. I would be interested in what you think would be the benefits and the drawbacks of moving in that direction.

Mr. KENDALL. Thank you. I am a little disappointed, Mr. Chairman, that the hearing yesterday was canceled when the chiefs were going to come over. I read all their testimony, and I have no issues with what they were going to say.

We have always supported that provision in the fiscal year 2016 NDAA. Having the chiefs more engaged in requirements tradeoffs and assessments of programs and actively engaged I think is very beneficial to the Department and to the services.

I have already met with each of the Service Chiefs, talked about the bill and how it affects them, and they are all off charging it— you know, how they would operate under that guidance.

It is a work in progress.

The only risk I see with it is that the chiefs are generally not experts in acquisition. They are experts in operational matters and requirements of leadership and so on. Their tendency is generally to try to go faster and get more and get it for less. We have gotten into a lot of trouble by making assumptions about how fast we could go and how much things would cost and how much they would do that prove out to be false.

One of the reasons my position exists is to provide a check and balance to that tendency. So I would still think that such a check and balance is needed, but the law does not remove that capability. So I am supportive of that provision and looking forward to working with the chiefs in their new role.

Senator HIRONO. Thank you very much.

Thank you, Mr. Chairman.

Chairman MCCAIN. Senator Ernst?

Senator ERNST. Thank you, Mr. Chair.

Thank you to Secretary James and Secretary Kendall for being here as well.

I think you have heard today we are all just very disappointed in the way the process has gone so far. We have an opportunity now to move forward in a different direction. So I am not going to hammer so much that, but the fact that I am assuming for decades the Air Force has known that the RD–180 could be withheld by the Russians at some point. So why is the solution just now being addressed? I would have thought this is something that should have been part of our discussion years and years and years ago. Can somebody explain that to me?

Mr. KENDALL. It actually has been part of our discussion. I think this predates Secretary James? return to the Department.

We have looked at budget issues to remove the dependency on the RD–180, but in the funding climate we have been in for the last several years, it has been unaffordable to the Department.

Now, when the Crimean events occurred, that all changed and it became obvious that we could no longer accept the risk of continued reliance on the RD–180. So I think we are all in agreement now that we need to get off of it as quickly as possible.

Prior to that point in time, we had consciously considered investing money to remove the RD–180 and develop a U.S. alternative, but it did not make the budget cuts, frankly, given the funding situation that we had.

Senator ERNST. Was that an issue of Congress or was that a departmental decision?

Mr. KENDALL. That was within the Department.

Senator ERNST. Should the Air Force have started a replacement engine program then long ago before it became so critical? Was that not a discussion that should have come to Congress?

Mr. KENDALL. With hindsight, we obviously should have. The expectation was that relationships with Russia after the end of the Cold War were going to be relatively benign. That has not turned out to be the case.

Senator ERNST. Just so we do not repeat this error in judgment—and I think we need to look at many of our acquisition programs and the way we do business across the board, not just this particular propulsion system, but we need to take some lessons learned here and move forward. Who in DOD, if anyone, should have been responsible for conducting the long-term planning and architectural development for the national security space enterprise including launch? Is there one person? Who is that? How is that structured?

Ms. JAMES. Well, I would say today if there is a single person, it would be me. I am, in addition to be Secretary of the Air Force, the principal defense space advisor. So that means my job is to, in a joint fashion, look not only at the Air Force but look at the entirety of our budgets because, of course, there is Army space, there is some Navy space as well to be able to work across the requirements community. I do not do all of this by myself. I do not mean to suggest that, but to be a single point of contact who can then make independent advice to the Secretary and Deputy Secretary.

Again, that is a new development. If you are going back in time, there probably were too many voices and no single independent voice that could reach across and provide that advice.

Senator ERNST. Are there communications now then between yourself and the other service branches?

Ms. JAMES. Yes, there are. I chair what is called the Defense Space Council. I am the principal advisor now to the Deputy and Secretary in terms of what we call the DMAG, which is where all of the important money discussions occur, as we are building our POM and finalizing our budget and so on. So there are additional authorities of late.

Senator ERNST. Can you describe that process then to me, because I am not familiar with that, how you do interact with the other services? Is this something we need to be aware of, any types of these situations that might happen with funding in the other branches as well?

Ms. JAMES. There certainly always crop up issues of policy and issues of funding across the Department of Defense. My role now as the principal defense space advisor is to stay well coordinated with the others, and even though at times I might be asked to go against my own Air Force budget, that is my job. That is my role to be able to rise above that and act in a joint way and be that independent voice.

Senator ERNST. Well, my time is running short, but I think communication is very key here. When these things do crop up, it is important that we engage Congress as well. We cannot let this happen again. You have spoken many times over about the American taxpayer. They expect much better from us. We have to do better. So lessons learned. We need to move forward at this point, and I think we need to develop our own technology as quickly as possible.

I thank you both for your time.

Thank you, Mr. Chairman.

Chairman MCCAIN. Senator Tillis?

Senator TILLIS. Thank you, Mr. Chair. Sorry about your Cardinals.

Chairman MCCAIN. Thanks for bringing that up.

[Laughter.]

Senator TILLIS. You know, first I share the frustration with the chair and the others that have spoken today. You know, it is amazing to me that creating this consistent capability since the time that we have started to where we are today has taken more time than the time between President Kennedy's aspiration to go the moon and getting to the moon.

My question, though, relates to something—and I am sorry. I have got a concurrent Judiciary Committee hearing going. It relates to the supply chain and the missions that we currently have planned either within DOD or outside of DOD. If we put all of our emphasis on a domestic launch capability, what sort of risk do we have in terms of important payloads where we are already in the chute to get them put into space? So what sort of risk do we have? Particularly I know some of the DOD missions you cannot talk about. I am just trying to get some sense of what are we looking at as a real shift to the right of many things that we want to get up into space sooner rather than later.

Ms. JAMES. The shifts to the right or the possible delays—I think I raised that as a detail that we would really have to think through carefully if we were to make the decision to stop all RD–180s and shift to have Delta on the one hand and the SpaceX on the other hand.

Senator TILLIS. I think as you go through that process, you should also look into the cost of delay because there is some inherent cost in having to carry those over and everything else that ripples through. I just think it is an important part of the decision-making process, while the real emphasis needs to be on getting that domestic capability. That is information we need sooner rather than later.

I know I have asked for some of it back when we were doing the NDAA. So I am hopeful that we can get that pretty quickly.

Mr. Chair, because I was out for most of the committee, I am not going to take any more time, but I did want to ask that question about getting the optics on the supply chain to us fairly quickly.

Chairman MCCAIN. Sorry you made it back.

[Laughter.]

Senator TILLIS. Go Panthers.

Chairman MCCAIN. Senator Rounds?

Senator ROUNDS. Thank you, Mr. Chairman.

Let me just walk my way back through this program to make sure that the background that we are all working with is consistent.

The intent originally, as I understand it, was that there was always going to be at least two organizations providing the delivery of our products into space. Originally we had two separate companies who then in 2006 joined together to create ULA. ULA then had two products, one from each of the two companies who they were at that time supporting, one being the Atlas V and also then the Delta IV, the Atlas V capable of intermediate lift capabilities, the Delta IV, the more expensive product, also capable of heavier lift capabilities.

Am I so far correct?

Ms. JAMES. Yes.

Senator ROUNDS. At the present time, you have then one organization now providing both of these products, but do both of these products not use commingling of parts in terms of their second stages? Even though we have got the RD–180 rocket under the Atlas, which is the Russian rocket motor, the Delta IV, being more expensive but also having more capabilities, both of them using the same products for their second stages and so forth. Is that correct? My understanding is that they are using the same product in both of those, or am I mistaken?

Mr. KENDALL. That is quite possible, but I do not know for certain if it is.

Senator ROUNDS. The reason why I ask is because I think we have always wanted the capability to have separate and independent supply lines, but if my suggestion is correct, we have had a single-source point for both of these two vehicles in other parts of the payload delivery systems.

Mr. KENDALL. Sir, I have not looked at that. That is something we could take a look at. I think if there are parts that are dual use, they are generally low-risk parts where we do not expect failures to occur, and they are parts that an instruction to an individual company could be replicated relatively easy. I am not certain of that. I need to go check.

Senator ROUNDS. Could you get back with us in terms of the second stage and so forth? The remaining part of this delivery product, as I understand it, has——

Mr. KENDALL. I understand. If there is a problem there, I am not aware of it. We would have to check.

[The information referred to follows:]

The Atlas V and Delta IV second stage designs are substantially different but share some similar components. One example is the Aerojet Rocketdyne RL–10 upper stage engine; variants of this engine are used on both Atlas V and Delta IV launch systems. The SpaceX Falcon 9 vehicle family, which was recently certified for use on Evolved Expendable Launch Vehicle launches, uses a completely different second stage engine relative to Atlas V and Delta IV reducing the concern over use of common and similar second stage components.

Senator ROUNDS. Okay.

Second question. I think Senator Cotton was on target when he started discussing about the fact that we wanted the assured access to space and at this time we believe that we have it. At the same time, we are talking about only intermediate delivery weights. If we are talking about heavy delivery weights, today we have only got one system out there and that is the Delta IV. Is that not correct?

So then how do we say that we have the assured access to space with regard to our heavier payloads?

Mr. KENDALL. The short answer is we do not. We would like to have that, but it has been prohibitively expensive. If SpaceX develops their heavy vehicle——

Senator ROUNDS. Excuse me. It would be consistent to say that we have the capability for intermediate payloads, but we do not for the heavier payloads at this time.

Mr. KENDALL. That is correct. One of the things we would like to be able to correct is that shortfall with future launch systems.

Senator ROUNDS. Well, but my understanding also is that the Delta IV, which is the product which ULA is currently proposing to phase out, is the only delivery system currently available for the heavier payloads. Is that not correct?

Mr. KENDALL. I believe that ULA is phasing out one variant of the Delta, and I do not believe it would preclude our launch. Is that correct?

Ms. JAMES. Correct.

Senator ROUNDS. Verify for me please. The Delta IV is——

Mr. KENDALL. Each of these rockets has different variants, and one of the variants of the Delta is being discontinued. ULA has announced they want to do that, but not all of them. I think it has not put our launches at risk.

Senator ROUNDS. So you will still have heavier lift capabilities.

Mr. KENDALL. Yes, I believe so.

Senator ROUNDS. Could you confirm that for the committee, please?

Mr. KENDALL. We will double check that, but I believe we would be all right.

Senator ROUNDS. Okay.

Another question on this. It seems to me that we now have two companies who at one time were competing with one another. They joined together in 2006. They have been since that time competing with two separate products but both of them they are responsible for. During this time, we have assumed that that provided us the assured access to space.

Now, we have got these two organizations together, ULA. We have been providing them with a base. I understand the concern the chairman has about $800 million a year, but I also understand that you want a consistent capability that is there and available on short notice.

My question to you, though, is this. This organization, while they have been buying product from Russia—and it appears that under our contracting program, we really did not care. We were looking the other way while they were using Russian rocket motors, the RD–180, during this time period because it was less expensive for us even though even back in the 1990s, there was a clear direction that if we ever used anything from the former Soviet Union, Defense Department policy clearly stated that it had to be phased out in 4 years. We appeared to just look the other way during this entire time frame?

Mr. KENDALL. You are correct about all that. "Look the other way" would probably be not the way I would characterize it.

Senator ROUNDS. You looked at it and just ignored it?

Mr. KENDALL. No. The way I would characterize is we accepted the risk associated with continuing to use the RD–180. As I said in response to Senator Ernst's question, there were conscious considerations of this situation in the Department. We were well aware of it, and we knew there was an element of risk associated with it. It was a multibillion dollar bill to build a clone of the RD–180 in the United States. In the tight budget environments we were in, that did not make the cut in the Department of Defense. It was consciously considered. With hindsight, obviously, we would like to have done something different, but we did not. So here we are.

Senator ROUNDS. Thank you, Mr. Chairman.

Chairman McCAIN. Senator King?

Senator KING. I apologize for missing some of the questions.

One of the pieces of analysis is the value to the taxpayers of a competitive launch versus using the Delta, which seems to be more expensive, if there is a lack of the 180s. Mr. Kendall, have you quantified that? What would the additional cost be?

Mr. KENDALL. Senator King, you put your finger on the question here. It is really a policy question of how much additional taxpayer money we should spend and how much risk we should take in the context of denying some income to the Russia oligarchs we have been talking about. That cost is on the order of tens of millions of dollars at least, and it depends upon how many launches and how much over a period of time. It also is a cost in delay, and it is a cost in risk in the viability of ULA if we go down that route. So there are a number of things there that weigh against moving in that direction.

There are things that weigh for it. Senator McCain is very eloquent about that. It is a policy decision. At the end of the day, the Department of Defense will do whatever the law directs us to do. If we are directed to get off the RD–180 today, we will do that, and we will do the best that we can without it. There are costs associated with that.

Senator KING. I would hope for the record you could perhaps give us some more detailed analysis. Is it tens of millions, hundreds of millions? Because that has to weigh into our decision.

Mr. KENDALL. It is at least tens of millions. Depending on how many launches were affected, how long it takes us to get to a more efficient source, it could be hundreds of millions, and it is delays that are measured probably in years. We could try to give you some more definitive information on that, though, if you would like.

Senator KING. I would appreciate that.

The second question is similar. As I understand it, there are a number of 180s in the pipeline that are approved under various discussions, but if we cut it off at different points, 9, 12, 14, 20, whatever, there could be a competitive gap. In other words, there could be a period of years where there is no alternative. Is that accurate? If so, what is that period? When does it start? When does it end?

Mr. KENDALL. We believe it would be several years before we could have a certified replacement for the RD–180. Our best estimates are that 2021 or so would be the time we could have a replacement. We would like to go faster. If we look at public-private partnerships, we would hope that some of those could go faster in terms of giving us a replacement. That is our best estimate right now.

Senator KING. Just because I am not sure what magnitude of dollars we are talking about, what does one of these rocket engines cost?

Mr. KENDALL. A medium launch is on the order of $100 million a launch. It is a good figure just to keep in your head.

Senator KING. That is the cost of the launch.

Mr. KENDALL. Yes.

Senator KING. I am talking about ULA. When they buy the rocket engine from Russia, what does it cost?

Mr. KENDALL. I believe the engine cost is on the order of—I am going to look to the people behind me. I think it is about $20 million. $30 million.

Senator KING. So $30 million is what we are talking about going to Russia. Of course, some significant part of that is the physical cost of building it. We do not know how much profit Brother Putin is making on those.

I really appreciate the analysis and look forward to that detailed analysis of the cost differential because I think that is an important consideration for us. Thank you very much for your testimony.

Thank you, Mr. Chairman.

Mr. KENDALL. Yes, sir. Thank you.

Chairman MCCAIN. I would like to point out to my colleague that both Blue Origin and SpaceX are developing and have had partial success with a reusable rocket engine. So that, of course, has a huge effect. There has been at least one success. So to somehow assume that it is going to be tens or hundreds of millions of dollars in extra costs ignores what these other non-ULA organizations are doing.

I am thinking now that we will have these various organizations that are not being subsidized for $800 million a year up before the committee. I will tell you in information they have conveyed to us, reusable rocket engines are certainly something they have had some success with. That changes the equation dramatically.

Senator KING. It changes it completely. I fully agree. Thank you.

Chairman MCCAIN. Senator Lee?

Senator LEE. Thank you, Mr. Chairman, for holding this hearing and for your attention to this important issue.

Thank you, Secretary James and Secretary Kendall, for being here to discuss this with us and for your service to our country.

I think we can all agree that in the coming years assured access to space is going to continue to be more and more important with each passing year. So I wanted to talk about what you think about the following question as we discuss both the short-term and the long-term considerations that have to be taken into account for a space launch. I am interested understanding how the Department of Defense and, to some extent, defense contractors might be looking toward the horizon for new, perhaps non-traditional forms of space launch technology that might be more cost-effective than our current technology.

So can you discuss any steps the Department might have taken to consider alternative forms of technology, such as advances in solid rocket motors? Do you believe that exploring new launch services, instead of just exploring new engines, might be the most effective way to end our reliance on Russian space launch technology?

Ms. JAMES. So I definitely believe, Senator, that we need to expand our horizon and keep focusing on the launch capability in its totality, of which the engine is a key component, but it is not the only component. So I will say that up front.

I will also say we are open to whatever types of—particularly this year with the NDAA written as it is, what other types of rocket propulsion systems in a full and open competitive way could lead to having new competitors and new capabilities to get us to space. That is what this is in part all about. Indeed, the solid motor application is one that there has been an award made under one of these other transaction authorities. So we are open to this.

There are fantastic developments in the commercial world. In my opening statement, I talked about how we are following them. We are celebrating them. We are putting some of our resources and time and energy toward trying to help them get there from here because we will all benefit from it. So totally open to it and one of the awards went in that direction.

Senator LEE. My understanding is that the market for these small payload launches is growing in the United States and it is also growing around the world. As you know, the Russians have been converting ICBM [intercontinental ballistic missile] motors into launch vehicles for smaller payload missions. This is kind of a low-cost approach that has attracted a lot of commercial users from around the world, a lot of customers from all over the world, including customers in the United States.

The Air Force, if I am not mistaken, stores more than 800 American ICBMs at a cost of about $17 million per year. At this point in time when the United States is trying to reduce our reliance on Russian companies for space launches and it is also trying to find savings within our defense budget, do you think that we could explore allowing domestic commercial use of our excess ICBM motors as long as proper inventory control measures were put in place? Is that a possibility?

Ms. JAMES. If you will allow me to go back and confirm that. Again, I am open to any of these new ideas. I do not believe, however, that those ICBM motors would have sufficient power to launch the types of satellites that we are talking about in our

EELV program, but perhaps there might be other applications that we should be thinking about. So if you will allow me to go back and explore that.

Senator LEE. Okay.

Secretary Kendall, you seem to be nodding. Do you want to add anything to that?

Mr. KENDALL. I am not aware of the possibilities there, but I think it is worth exploring. I think, as Secretary James indicated, it would be for smaller launches.

We do want to exploit the technologies that are in development like the ones Senator McCain mentioned. We want those investments to be part of a path to assured launch service providers, and that is the distinction between just spending money on propulsion and hoping that these commercial ventures are successful and ultimately give us what we need or actually getting on a contractual path that gets us there for sure and provides the services that we need. That is the difference between the two approaches we have been talking about.

Senator LEE. Right, right. So it is not just about the motors. It is also with the launch services. I would appreciate any information you can get back to me on that as a follow-up. Assuming there are some that would work, I question whether it would make sense to prohibit American launch providers from purchasing excess ICBM motors for commercial use while allowing Russians to take all of the business in that market, assuming there would be a market there.

Thank you both and thank you, Mr. Chairman.

Chairman MCCAIN. Senator Shaheen I am told is on her way back. So I will just mention a couple things.

We are going to have the various organizations that are developing these new technologies, including reusable rocket engines and others, before the committee.

For the record, Secretary Kendall, you have said that it costs tens of millions, hundreds of millions of dollars extra if we just went with the Atlas rocket. I would like a much more definitive answer as to how much those additional costs are in your view.

By the way, I am confident that one of these outfits is going to develop a reasonable rocket engine. They have already had success and they predict it. That then, of course, changes your estimates rather dramatically. That is why we need them before the committee.

Jeff, did you have any additional questions or comments?

Senator SESSIONS. No. Thank you, Mr. Chairman.

Your goal, our goal I think of the committee would be to create a competitive environment where two or more innovative, creative American-based companies are producing our essential launch systems. I think we all agree on that. The sooner, the better.

With regard to the $800 million, there are costs for maintaining, Secretary Kendall, the launch systems and the pads and all of that, but in the future, the way you are proposing it, everybody that bids, whether it is SpaceX or Blue Origin or ULA—they would explicitly put in their bid that cost. Is that the way they would do it?

Mr. KENDALL. We are phasing out that contract, and I do not foresee us using that type of contract again.

Senator SESSIONS. They would just have to bid in there—I mean, they would have to include in their proposal probably the cost of maintaining a launch pad and all——

Mr. KENDALL. Yes, they would. For that reason, we made the adjustment to the current contract so that there is no effective subsidy of ULA any longer.

Senator SESSIONS. I do think the Senator is right. My best judgment is we are in a transformative time. It would be great. SpaceX is out there doing some great work. I think Blue Origin has great capabilities, and others are talking about some plans that could work too.

So thank you, Mr. Chairman.

Chairman MCCAIN. Well, thank you.

I would just point out my rough estimate between 2005–2016—that is about $7.2 billion we have paid ULA—that math may be wrong—for staying in business. There is plenty of corporations that do business with the Defense Department we do not pay $800 million a year just to stay in business. They do research. They do development. They do testing. They do work. This $800 million a year, and then not even bid on a launch. You talk about in your face.

I am sorry. I do not think we can wait much longer.

Go ahead.

Senator REED. Just let me make a brief statement.

First, thank you, Mr. Chairman. I think the hearing has been very, very insightful.

If Senator Shaheen—I will immediately yield to her if she arrives.

Just one of the things that was revealed in the hearing is the complexity of all these issues. One aspect of this, for want of a better term, is reliability because a lot of this effort began in the late 1990s when we suffered a series of significant setbacks, not only billions of dollars of equipment, but intelligence capabilities that were absolutely critical and vital were lost.

I do not know what the scientific correlation is but innovation is—there is a little tradeoff between reliability and innovation in sort of a street-wise sense. So I just want to simply say that that is one of the aspects that I think we have to look at.

This has been a very important hearing, and the chairman's leadership has been I think in exactly the right direction. We are all sitting here saying we have got to stop buying RD–180s, do it smartly and do it quickly. That is the point the chairman has made repeatedly.

Chairman MCCAIN. We cannot impose on the time of the witnesses any longer. My regrets to Senator Shaheen.

This hearing is adjourned. I thank the witnesses.

[Whereupon, at 11:03 a.m., the hearing was adjourned.]

[Questions for the record with answers supplied follow:]

MILITARY SPACE LAUNCH AND THE USE OF RUSSIAN-MADE ROCKET ENGINES

It has come to my attention that payments for RD–180 rocket engines may be made to the Russian company NPO Energomash in United States dollars (USD) through the middle-man RD AMROSS. Since the Russian invasion of Crimea nearly two years ago, this financial arrangement has become even more lucrative for the Russians due to the unprecedented strength of the USD against the ruble.

1. Senator GRAHAM. Is it accurate that these transactions are made in USD?
Secretary KENDALL. The Department purchases launch services, not launch vehicle hardware. The Air Force's contracts with United Launch Alliance (ULA) are for launch services utilizing the Atlas V launch vehicle. These contracts specify amounts in USD. The subcontracts between ULA and RD AMROSS for purchase of the RD–180 engines specify amounts in USD. However, how ULA subcontractor RD AMROSS pays their vendor NPO Energomash for the manufacture of the RD–180 engines should be addressed with ULA and RD AMROSS.

2. Senator GRAHAM. Are foreign transactions usually done in USD? If so, is there anything that can be done to stop this type of transaction which appears to greatly benefit the Russian Government?
Secretary KENDALL. The Department does not procure nor pay for the RD–180 rocket engines directly from a foreign supplier. The prime contractor, United Launch Alliance (ULA), pays its suppliers for space launch rocket components. Both ULA contracts with RD AMROSS and RD AMROSS contracts with NPO Energomash are specified and paid in USD. Absent suspension, debarment, statutory restriction, or a Presidential Executive Order sanction on contracting with a prohibited source, defense contractors would not be precluded from using normal commercial financing and payment terms with their suppliers.

Senator GRAHAM. I understand that the BE–4 engine under development will use liquefied natural gas (LNG) as its propellant instead of kerosene as is used in the Russian RD–180. I also understand that ULA is pursuing an entirely new rocket, the Vulcan that will use LNG. The use of LNG as a fuel, some experts have advised, may require launch pad modifications as well as other new infrastructure and equipment.
3. Are you aware that significant changes to the launch pad and other modifications may be required if an LNG engine is used in the Vulcan?
Secretary KENDALL. Yes, the Department is aware that if the BE–4 engine is selected as the propulsion system for the ULA Vulcan launch vehicle there will be a requirement for some launch pad modifications.

4. Senator GRAHAM. Have the additional funds been taken into account in the Department's future budget estimates?
Secretary KENDALL. The Department purchases launch services and does not directly invest in infrastructure that is required to perform the required service. Funding for infrastructure development is generally the responsibility of the launch service provider.
If, however, United Launch Alliance is selected to enter into a public-private partnership with the Department as part of the Next Generation Launch System Investment activity, it is possible that some of the funding the Department has requested in the Fiscal Year 2017 President's Budget could be used to support launch pad modification for the Vulcan program.

5. Senator GRAHAM. Who will be responsible to pay for these additional launch pad modifications and additional infrastructure?
Secretary KENDALL. In general, the Department purchases launch services and does not directly invest in infrastructure that is required to perform the required service. Funding for infrastructure development is generally the responsibility of the launch service provider.
If, however, United Launch Alliance is selected to enter into a public-private partnership with the Department as part of the Next Generation Launch System Investment activity, it is possible that some of the funding the Department has requested in the Fiscal Year 2017 President's Budget could be used to support launch pad modification for the Vulcan program.

Senator GRAHAM. You testified that current estimates for replacing the RD–180 rocket engine would be about $3 billion. That estimate greatly exceeds what some industry experts believe will be needed for development and integration of a new rocket engine.

6. In order to understand your analysis better, please provide an accounting of your $3 billion estimate.

Secretary KENDALL. The Department's preferred approach for transitioning from the RD–180 engine is to invest, via public private partnerships, in launch service development and not to develop a replacement engine. An engine by itself does not provide the launch capability needed for national security space satellites. My testimony presented a very rough estimate for an engine program by itself. This engine program cost would include development and qualification engine hardware, refurbishing test stands, integration costs with the launch vehicle, and a demonstration launch late in the program. This program cost did not include potential costs for the use of Delta IV launch vehicles on planned Atlas V missions in the transition period.

————————

QUESTIONS SUBMITTED BY SENATOR JACK REED

NUMBER OF RD–180 ENGINES

Senator REED. There has been a lot of debate concerning the number of RD–180 engines we will need. My understanding is the current Falcon 9.1 cannot lift all the satellites the Atlas can using the RD–180 engine. This leaves a possible gap until some sort of replacement rocket for the Atlas comes on line.

7. Is this gap in lift accurate and how many RD–180 engines do we need for the Atlas, for how long and why?

Secretary JAMES. We need assured access to space. If we are no longer allowed to use RD–180s, we may be forced to use more Deltas at a higher cost which is not in our budget. If United Launch Alliance (ULA) retires the Delta IV in the fiscal year 2018 timeframe as they have announced and the Atlas V becomes unavailable due to the RD–180 restrictions, there will be a gap in assured access to space as well as a gap in competition for National Security Space (NSS) launch missions, during which time the SpaceX Falcon 9 Upgrade, the SpaceX Falcon 9 Heavy (when certified), and the Delta IV Heavy launch vehicles become the only means of spacelift. As indicated last year, we believe authorization to use up to 18 RD–180 engines is a reasonable starting point for the transition timeframe. There are approximately 34 competitive launch service opportunities/procurements during the fiscal year 2015–fiscal year 2022 timeframe. Use of the RD–180 mitigates risk associated with assured access to space and enables competition.

SPLIT BUYS

Senator REED. At times to preserve our industrial base, services such as the Navy have used an acquisition approach called dual allocation, which allocates set quantities to two providers.

8. Do think such an approach is feasible between SpaceX and ULA if ULA were to retain the Delta IV until such time as a replacement for the Atlas IV is developed?

Secretary JAMES. A dual allocation approach between SpaceX and ULA is feasible. The Air Force is investigating several acquisition strategy approaches to preserve assured access to space and foster competition. One potential strategy is an allocation approach for Evolved Expendable Launch Vehicle (EELV) Phase 2 launch service procurements. Based on initial Air Force estimates, it would cost DOD in excess of $1.5B more to allocate between Falcon and Delta IV without access to the Atlas V launch vehicle. This cost estimate assumes there is no access to RD–180 engines for the 28 projected EELV Phase 2 missions during the fiscal year 2018–fiscal year 2022 timeframe. For the 28 Phase 2 missions, the Air Force estimate assumes an even allocation of 14 missions for the Delta IV and 14 missions for the Falcon 9 based on discussions with the SASC staff.

9. Senator REED. How much added cost would this be (and why) until 2022 at which time ULA is supposed to have certified a new launch system to replace the Atlas?

Secretary JAMES. The Air Force is investigating several acquisition strategy approaches to preserve assured access to space and foster competition. One potential strategy is an allocation approach for Evolved Expendable Launch Vehicle (EELV) Phase 2 launch service procurements. Based on initial Air Force estimates, it would cost DOD in excess of $1.5B more to allocate between Falcon and Delta IV without access to the Atlas V launch vehicle. This cost estimate assumes there is no access to RD–180 engines for the 28 projected EELV Phase 2 missions during the fiscal year 2018–fiscal year 2022 timeframe. For the 28 Phase 2 missions, the Air Force estimate assumes an even allocation of 14 missions for the Delta IV and 14 missions for the Falcon 9 based on discussions with the SASC staff.

LIQUID ROCKET ENGINE INDUSTRIAL BASE

Senator REED. If ULA were to cease production of the Delta IV purely for competitive reasons it would eliminate production of the RS–68 engine produced by Rocketdyne—our only U.S. company solely focused on liquid propellant rocket engines for medium and heavy lift. NASA relies on Rocketdyne to produce engines as well for their Space Launch System, the RS–25.

10. What is your assessment of the impact to Rocketdyne if ULA were to cease production of the Delta IV engine?

Secretary KENDALL. Based on Aerojet Rocketdyne (AR) financial reporting to the Security and Exchange Commission, ULA represents approximately 20 percent of AR's business base. This includes the Delta IV RS–68 engine, the RL–10 upper stage engine which flies on both the Atlas V and Delta IV vehicles, the Atlas V solid rocket boosters (SRB), and some development activities on the AR–1 main stage engine. In 2015, ULA competed its contract for SRBs and awarded the contract to Orbital ATK. As a result, AR will cease providing SRBs to ULA in 2018. If Delta IV production ends, a significant portion of AR's revenue could be lost as RS–68 production will be terminated, approximately 13 percent of their overall liquid rocket engine revenue, and production of the RL–10 will be reduced. Further, a Delta IV production stop also has the potential to impact the NASA RS–25D/E production restart program in the form of increased overhead rates. Should United Launch Alliance, as a launch system integrator, select the AR–1 as the mainstage propulsion system for its next generation Vulcan-Centaur rocket, the loss of revenue from the RS–68 could somewhat be mitigated.

INTERPRETATION OF FISCAL YEAR 2016 NDAA AND SECTION 8048 OF THE FISCAL YEAR 2016 OMNIBUS APPROPRIATIONS ACT

Senator REED. As you know there are two provisions addressing the competition for DOD launch that have become law for fiscal year 2016. One is section 1607 of the Fiscal Year 2016 NDAA permitting the purchase of 4 additional RD–180 engines beyond the existing 36 core block buy with ULA and one in the section 8048 of the Fiscal Year 2016 Omnibus Appropriations Act permitting any DOD "certified" provider of launch to compete—regardless of engine origin.

11. What is your interpretation of these two provisions taken together?

Secretary KENDALL. Based on the Department's review, we believe the two provisions can be read together so that there is no inconsistency as they are applied to the present Air Force fiscal year 2016 procurement plan. If the Air Force plans to contract for launch services with Atlas RD–180 engines for up to four engines, both statutes would authorize such a plan. However, if the Air Force plans to contract for launch services in Fiscal Year 2016 with more than four Atlas RD–180 engines, we believe section 8048 of the Fiscal Year 2016 Omnibus Appropriations Act takes precedence to authorize such use of RD–180 engines.

RD–180 ENGINE REPLACEMENT EFFORT

Senator REED. You have the rare circumstance where the Congress is appropriating more funds than you have requested—specifically for the replacement of the RD–180, the Congress has appropriated in the past two years about $300 million more than requested for this effort.

12. Are you able to achieve the goal of the Fiscal Year 2015 NDAA to have a replacement by 2019 and if not why?

Secretary JAMES. Our engine experts have said that the timeline to get an engine by 2019 is very aggressive and challenging. It is possible to get an engine by 2019, but an engine alone does not get you to space. More time is needed to integrate the engine into a launch system. An independent review led by Gen (ret) Mitchell looked closely at this problem and gathered inputs from across both government and commercial industry. The team estimated that it would take approximately six years to build an engine from a cold start. As an example, the original RS–68 (Delta IV engine) development took eight years to get to first launch and cost ~$750M. The RS–68A upgrade development took six years and cost ~$250M.

QUESTIONS SUBMITTED BY SENATOR KELLY AYOTTE

COST OF LAUNCHES

13. Senator AYOTTE. Secretary James and Secretary Kendall: Is ULA pursuing innovations with the Delta IV, Atlas V, or the Atlas successor that have the potential to achieve cost-competitiveness in a reusable vehicle marketplace?

Secretary JAMES. ULA is looking to transition from its legacy launch families, Delta IV and Atlas V, to its next generation launch family which is called Vulcan. It is the Air Force's understanding that ULA is evaluating ways to be competitive with Vulcan in the dynamic launch vehicle marketplace.

Secretary KENDALL. ULA has publicly stated that the reason for the shutdown of the Delta vehicle line and the transition from Atlas V to the Vulcan vehicle is to achieve cost competitiveness in the evolving launch service marketplace. ULA has also publicly indicated that they are exploring the cost effectiveness of adding a limited engine reusability capability to the evolving Vulcan design.

14. Senator AYOTTE. Are those sorts of innovations things that the Air Force is looking at while managing its booking of launches?

Secretary JAMES. The Air Force continues to foster competition and work with industry to certify new launch providers for our National Security Space (NSS) payloads. The Air Force has developed a cogent set of source selection criteria for deciding which certified launch provider will be chosen to launch each mission. The Air Force's strategy of full and open competition is intended to foster innovative approaches.

Secretary KENDALL. The Department awards launch service contracts only to certified launch providers that meet the requirements for specific missions. If an innovative solution is presented by a launch service provider, it would be considered as long as the innovation does not change the provider's certified baseline. Any innovations outside the certified baseline would drive a vehicle re-certification. While the Air Force encourages innovation, our highest priority is assured access to space using reliable launch services.

HEAVY LIFT LAUNCHES

15. Senator AYOTTE. If phasing out the Delta IV medium-lift variant makes the Heavy variant more expensive, why is the Air Force supporting ULA's decision to phase out the Delta IV and rely on the Atlas V?

Secretary JAMES. The Air Force procures launch services and does not control United Launch Alliance's (ULA) internal business decisions. ULA's decisions to phase out the Delta IV and rely on the Atlas V are due to Delta IV's lack of cost competitiveness. The Air Force has funded ULA to analyze the cost impacts of retaining the Delta IV single core for National Security Space missions.

Secretary KENDALL. The Department's goal is to have at least two commercially viable launch service providers that utilize domestic rocket propulsion systems and meet all National Security Space (NSS) requirements. ULA has publicly stated that it made a business decision to eliminate all the Delta Medium and Medium+ variants in an effort to restructure its business in order to ensure it remains a viable launch service provider. The Air Force has not taken a position on whether or not this is a sound business decision.

16. Senator AYOTTE. If we had no more access to RD–180s immediately, could we instead shift Atlas V resources as we use existing RD–180 stock to the Delta IV and maintain our medium-lift assured access to space (with Delta IV and Falcon 9) and also preserve our current one-vehicle heavy lift capacity (with Delta IV Heavy)? Would that save taxpayer dollars?

Secretary JAMES. United Launch Alliance (ULA) has committed to maintaining the Delta IV Heavy capability as long as National Security Space (NSS) has a requirement for the vehicle, which will be at least until 2022. ULA has civil and commercial Atlas V missions. By shifting Atlas V NSS resources to Delta IV, we would cause the fixed costs allocation to those missions remaining on Atlas V to increase, thus jeopardizing the commercial viability of Atlas V and ULA's ability to support development of the Vulcan launch system. In addition, Tori Bruno, CEO of ULA, publicly stated at the HASC Strategic Forces Subcommittee hearing on June 26, 2015 that it costs 35 percent more to build a Delta IV launch vehicle than an Atlas V. Based on initial estimates, it would cost DOD in excess of $1.5B more to implement a Falcon 9 and Delta IV only approach for Evolved Expendable Launch Vehicle (EELV) Phase 2 (launch procurement in fiscal year 2018–2022).

Secretary KENDALL. If access to RD–180 engines were immediately cut off, the Department would work with ULA to evaluate the current inventory of RD–180s available for the Department's use and determine which National Security Space (NSS) missions, if any, to transfer to the appropriately-sized Delta IV. We would also work with SpaceX to determine availability and capability of Falcon vehicles. First, this re-manifesting to Delta IV and Falcon 9 would delay the launch of critical NSS missions. Second, the Department would incur not only reintegration costs but also storage costs due to the schedule delays. For each mission transferred to a Delta vehicle, a minimum of a 30 percent increase in individual mission costs should be expected. Today, the Falcon Upgrade launch vehicle is only certified to launch into four of the eight EELV required orbits. If this situation were to occur, the Department could expect an overall significant increase in the cost of launch to the Government over the Future Years Defense Program.

WHY MOVING SO SLOW?—WENT TO MOON MUCH FASTER

17. Senator AYOTTE. When is the earliest that we can develop a domestic rocket engine that can be integrated into the Atlas V?

Secretary JAMES. Our engine experts have said that the timeline to get an engine by 2019 is very aggressive and challenging. It is possible to get an engine by 2019, but an engine alone does not get you to space. More time is needed to integrate the engine into a launch system. We believe the 2022/2023 timeframe is the earliest a new engine integrated with a launch vehicle can be certified and ready for flight. An independent review led by Maj Gen Howard J. Mitchell (USAF–Ret) looked closely at this problem and gathered inputs from across both government and commercial industry. The team estimated that it would take approximately 6 years to build an engine from a cold start. As an example, the original RS–68 (Delta IV engine) development took eight years to get to first launch and cost ~$750M. The RS–68A upgrade development took six years and cost ~$250M.

Secretary KENDALL. The Department wants to end use of the RD–180 as soon as possible but does not believe this can be accomplished before 2021 or 2022. To be clear, the Department does not intend to unilaterally pay for the development of a direct replacement engine for the RD–180 on the Atlas V. The costs would be excessive to the Department, and a specific engine program would only benefit one launch service provider.

The Department's goal is competitive public-private partnerships with commercial launch service providers that result in new and improved launch service capabilities. This is the quickest and most efficient way to get off the RD–180.

18. Senator AYOTTE. What does it say to you about the state of our nation's defense industrial base and our acquisition system that it took less time in the 1960s to build the rocket that took us to the moon than it will take to build a new rocket engine today?

Secretary JAMES. The earliest test firings of components that became part of the Saturn V first-stage F–1 engine took place in 1957. The first manned Saturn V flight—the Apollo 8 circumlunar mission (the first lunar orbit mission)—occurred in December 1968. This represents a decade-long development cycle.

With appropriate and sustained funding for engine development as part of an integrated launch system, as was the case with the F–1 and Saturn V, our nation's defense industrial base and our acquisition system could conceivably equal or surpass the achievements of the Saturn V example.

Secretary KENDALL. The F–1 engine that powered the rocket system that took us to the moon began development in 1955 and first flew in 1967. The development of new propulsion and associated launch systems for the Evolved Expendable Launch Vehicle (EELV) program will require about five to seven years and remains one of the most challenging design and development activities the Nation pursues, as flawless technical performance is paramount. The Department remains committed to ending the use of the RD–180 engine as soon as possible while still maintaining the Nation's assured access to space. We plan on doing this in the most prudent but expeditious manner possible.

19. Senator AYOTTE. Is it true that you did not release contracts for the development of a prototype engine until just a couple weeks ago?

Secretary JAMES. After the Fiscal Year 2015 NDAA was passed in December 2014, the Air Force released the Request for Proposals (RFP) for the Booster Propulsion Technology Maturation Project Broad Agency Announcement (BAA) on June 2, 2015. After a full and open competition, the Air Force awarded the first BAA contract on November 4, 2015. The Air Force has awarded a total of ten contracts

($34.6M) under the BAA. These Booster Propulsion Tech Maturation Project BAA awards continue the strategy to transition off the RD–180 with a launch service approach. Specifically, they support the Fiscal Year 2015 Authorization and Appropriation Acts' direction to initiate engine risk reduction and technology maturation efforts to develop a next-generation rocket propulsion system. Separately, the Air Force released an innovative public-private partnership RFP on June 2, 2015 for investment in industry's rocket propulsion systems through full and open competition. The Air Force initiated rocket propulsion system development partnerships with industry on January 13, 2016 with the award of the first two Other Transaction Authority agreements ($80.5M). The final two of four Other Transaction Authority agreements were awarded on February 29, 2016 ($141.6M).

Secretary KENDALL. It is true that four Other Transaction Authority agreements for the Rocket Propulsion System project were recently awarded following source selection and congressional notification. Two were awarded January 13, 2016: one to SpaceX for a single project and one to Orbital ATK for three projects. Two more were awarded on February 29, 2016: one to Aerojet Rocketdyne for a single project and one to United Launch Alliance for two projects.

20. Senator AYOTTE. What took so long? It has been almost two years since Russia invaded Ukraine's Crimea.

Secretary JAMES. Since the Fiscal Year 2015 NDAA was passed in December 2014, the Air Force released the Request for Proposals (RFP) for the Booster Propulsion Technology Maturation Project Broad Agency Announcement (BAA) on June 2, 2015. After a full and open competition, the Air Force awarded the first BAA contract on November 4, 2015. The Air Force has awarded a total of ten contracts ($34.6M) under the BAA. These Booster Propulsion Tech Maturation Project BAA awards continue the strategy to transition off the RD–180 with a launch service approach. Specifically, they support the Fiscal Year 2015 Authorization and Appropriation Acts' direction to initiate engine risk reduction and technology maturation efforts to develop a next-generation rocket propulsion system. Separately, the Air Force released an innovative public-private partnership RFP on June 2, 2015 for investment in industry's rocket propulsion systems through full and open competition. The Air Force initiated rocket propulsion system development partnerships with industry on January 13, 2016 with the award of the first two Other Transaction Authority agreements ($80.5M). The final two of four Other Transaction Authority agreements were awarded on February 29, 2016 ($141.6M).

Secretary KENDALL. The release of these Rocket Propulsion System (RPS) Other Transaction Agreements (OTAs) is actually only the most recent portion of a multiple-year process that includes model development and technology maturation activities. These activities will result in new and improved launch services capabilities for the Department. In August 2014, the Air Force released a Booster Propulsion and Launch Systems Request for Information to obtain more detailed information regarding each domestic space launch service and rocket propulsion provider's proposed new or modified launch system(s), including the technical development plans and business cases. The first funding supporting the overall RPS activities was obligated for subscale testing in November 2014. In addition, a total of 10 Broad Area Announcement awards were made in CY 2015 and early CY 2016. The OTAs that were awarded in January 2016 were followed by additional RPS awards in February following required congressional notification. As requested in the Fiscal Year 2017 President's Budget, the final step in the Department's transition away from the RD–180 will be the release of a Draft Request for Proposals for the Government Launch Service Investment portion of the process that will result in new and improved launch service capabilities, powered by American-made rocket engines, for the Department and the Nation.

SPENDING TAX DOLLAR ON U.S. PROTECTIVE EQUIPMENT

Senator AYOTTE. The United States Government, through DOD, continues to support many allies who are fighting terrorism around the world. Part of that support comes from direct funding and FMF dollars given to specific nations that are designated to be spent on properly outfitting their warfighters with quality protective equipment and combat clothing. This equipping effort provides the opportunity to ensure that our allies have the essential combat clothing and body armor needed to maximize our allies' safety and performance, while strengthening the U.S. defense industrial base.

21. Which laws or regulations do you believe govern whether those FMF funds must be spent in the United States?

Secretary KENDALL. The permanent authority for financing the procurement of defense articles, defense services, and design and construction services by friendly foreign countries and international organizations is section 23 of the Arms Export Control Act (AECA) of 1976, as amended, title 22, U.S.C section 2763. Other provisions of the AECA restrict financed sales in the case of coproduction or licensed production outside of the United States (AECA section 42(b)) and restrict use of funds outside of the United States only upon determination that the procurement will not result in adverse effects on the U.S. economy or industrial mobilization base. AECA section 42(c) states that the determination must consider the balance between impacts on labor surplus areas and the balance of U.S. payments with the rest of the world against economic and other advantages to the United States for procurement outside of the United States. The authority to make this determination has been delegated to the Director, DSCA, in the Department of Defense, with concurrence from the Department of State and the Department of Commerce.

To carry out section 23 of the AECA, FMF funds are appropriated in the annual Department of State, Foreign Operations, and Related Programs Appropriations Act. The Appropriations Acts contain recurring provisions that allow the Government of Israel to use a portion of its FMF allocation for procurements in Israel. The Acts also contain restrictions on making FMF available for procurement of defense articles, services, and design and construction services that are not sold by the U.S. Government.

The Cargo Preference Act of 1954 as amended, title 46, U.S.C., section 55305, requires at least 50 percent of the gross tonnage (computed separately for dry bulk carriers, dry cargo liners, and tankers) of FMF-funded cargo be transported in privately-owned U.S. flag vessels to the extent such vessels are available at fair and reasonable rates as determined by the Maritime Administration (MARAD). DSCA, in support of the U.S. maritime industry, requires 100 percent of applicable cargoes to be carried by U.S. flag vessels unless a general or security waiver is granted by DSCA or a non-availability waiver is granted by MARAD.

22. Senator AYOTTE. How does DOD ensure compliance with those laws and regulations?

Secretary KENDALL. DOD works closely with the Department of State to submit to the Congress the Annual Classified Budget Justification Annex for Foreign Appropriations, which includes an annual detailed breakout of the proposed country FMF programs. This report is released annually in the June timeframe to Congress and updated regularly throughout the year. DOD and State work together to ensure FMF funds are spent for the purposes that are provided to Congress. Off-shore procurements using FMF are not approved unless the circumstances justify a determination permitting off-shore procurement with FMF funds under section 42(c) of the Arms Export Control Act. The DSCA Security Assistance Management Manual (SAMM) at C9.7.2.7.3 describes the process for considering requests for off-shore procurement using FMF funds. SAMM C7.7.1 describes in general terms the application of the Cargo Preference Act for shipping of defense articles procured with FMF funds.

QUESTIONS SUBMITTED BY SENATOR DAN SULLIVAN

ALASKAN F–35S

23. Senator SULLIVAN. In about a month, the Air Force should reach a Record of Decision ("ROD") on the basing of the F–35 at Eielson AFB. When will the ROD be officially announced?

Secretary JAMES. The ROD was officially announced on 4 April 2016.

24. Senator SULLIVAN. How confidant are you that the two squadrons of F–35s will in fact be based at Eielson AFB, and what is the timeline for all of the aircraft, maintenance manning, and support arrive at these two squadrons?

Secretary JAMES. On 30 Jul 14, the Secretary of the Air Force identified Eielson AFB as the preferred alternative for the second operational F–35 location. The notice of availability for the final Environmental Impact Statement (EIS) was published in the Federal Register on 4 Mar 16 for 30 day public comment.

The Air Force signed the record of decision finalizing the basing action on 4 April, announcing initial aircraft arrival in 2020.

Senator SULLIVAN. By the summer of 2020, two squadrons of F–35s should have attained full operational capability at Eielson AFB. As you have stated, Close Air Support will be a primary mission of the F–35.

25. What steps is the Air Force taking to ensure that the F–35s at Eielson will integrate with the US Army and synergize their Close Air Support training objectives?

Secretary JAMES. Currently the 3rd Air Support Operations Squadron (ASOS) at Joint Base Elmendorf-Richardson, and the 3rd ASOS DET 1 at Fort Wainwright, AK provide a liaison between Air Force and the Army units stationed in Alaska. The Air Force will continue to execute daily training interactions, as well as major exercises such as Red Flag and Distant Frontier to integrate Close Air Support Training between U.S. Air Force and Army units in Alaska.

26. Senator SULLIVAN. What ground-based and air-based electronic warfare improvements are going to be made to the JPARC in order to maintain a robust and realistic training environment for daily integration of Alaska's F–35s and F–22s, as well as other joint and coalition partners?

Secretary JAMES. The JPARC is one of the Air Force's most robust and costly ranges with a total of 27 threat emitters, supported by the U.S. Air Force, which represent a broad range of Surface to Air capabilities. The Air Force recognizes the current threat inventory across the range enterprise does not fully replicate enemy threat radar waveforms and parametric signatures. As such, the Air Force is investing in the development of two Advanced Radar Threat Systems (ARTS v1 and v2), which will represent strategic and tactical systems in order to better replicate adversary capabilities. These systems are in the beginning phases of acquisition and will be added to JPARC's inventory when fielded. The Air Force is also working with industry to modernize and upgrade the current threat simulator fleet to quickly replicate current and future enemy systems. JPARC also has 15 former Soviet Union widely proliferated threats that cannot be modified or upgraded through the AF acquisition process. However, 8 of the 27 threat emitters, supported by the U.S. Air Force, will be included in the modernization plan over the next four years. The result will be a broad range of threat capabilities that provides a full array of near-peer capabilities.

Senator SULLIVAN. Given that Alaska will have two squadrons of F–35s, two squadrons of F–22s—nearly 100 5th Generation fighters—in addition to the Eielson Aggressors and a robust electronic warfare training range in the JPARC.

27. Is it fair to say that Alaska has emerged as a hub of 5th Generation combat airpower and training for the USAF and the DOD at large?

Secretary JAMES. The Alaska training ranges and airspace indeed provide a wide variety of training opportunities for U.S. Air Force, Joint, and Coalition partners. The proximity of F–22 and F–35 units in Alaska, along with the JPARC range and Alaskan airspaces and our aggressor units, will significantly advance our opportunities to integrate 4th and 5th Generation airpower in high-end large force exercises and training.

Senator SULLIVAN. Alaska sits in a critical strategic location, and is the crucible where NORTHCOM, EUCOM, and PACOM all intersect. It carries a 24/7 alert mission to counter increased Russian aggression, has embedded strategic airlift with the C–17 and C–130s at JBER, and will eventually host 4 squadrons of the World's only 5th Generation fighters.

28. With these critical nation security assets in such an enabling strategic location, does it make sense to base the KC–46 tanker in Alaska to add to these capabilities?

Secretary JAMES. The Air Force uses its deliberate, repeatable and standardized strategic basing process to determine the locations best suited to support any given mission. Should the Air Force pursue KC–46 basing in the Pacific Air Forces (PACAF) area of responsibility, we will use the basing process to determine the location.

QUESTIONS SUBMITTED BY SENATOR BILL NELSON

EFFECT ON DEFENSE DEPARTMENT ACCESS TO SPACE

29. Senator NELSON. What effect would the combination of an immediate ban on the use of Russian-made engines and early termination of the current EELV Launch Capability (ELC) contract have on Defense Department access to space, cost to the

department for future launches, and on the U.S. commercial launch industry as a whole?

Secretary KENDALL. These two events would have a serious negative effect on the Department's ability to support the Warfighter by providing the timely launch of critical space assets.

If access to RD–180 engines were immediately cut off, the Department would work with United Launch Alliance (ULA) to evaluate the current inventory of RD–180s available for the Department's use and determine which National Security Space (NSS) missions, if any, to transfer to the appropriately sized Delta IV. We would also work with SpaceX to determine availability and capability of Falcon vehicles. First, this re-manifesting to Delta IV and Falcon 9 would delay the launch of critical NSS missions. Second, the Department would incur not only reintegration costs but also storage costs due to the schedule delays. Finally, in the short term, for each mission transferred to a Delta vehicle, a minimum of a 30 percent increase in individual mission costs should be expected. Today, the Falcon Upgrade launch vehicle is only certified to launch into four of the eight EELV required orbits.

The early termination of the ELC portion of the EELV contract combined with the loss of access to the RD–180 engine could require a renegotiation of the Air Force EELV "block buy" contract with ULA. At a minimum, this could potentially expose the Department to a Request for Equitable Adjustment (REA) from ULA and, depending on the circumstances, the REA could result in significant additional expense to the Government.

Such a disruption could threaten the Nation's assured access to space and drive the Department into a near-term segmented sole source environment with Delta IV with ULA and Falcon 9 Upgrade with SpaceX.

Secretary JAMES. The combination of immediately banning the use of Russian-made engines and early termination of the current EELV Launch Capability (ELC) portion of the Phase 1 contract, FA8811–13–C–0003 (a.k.a. Block Buy) would significantly disrupt National Security Space (NSS) launch.

The Block Buy contract has two main elements. The first element, Launch Vehicle Production Services (LVPS), focuses on the hardware and touch labor to build the rocket. The second element, ELC, focuses on the infrastructure and critical skills to launch the rocket. These elements of cost are inherent to any and all launch services. If the ELC Fiscal Year 2017 option is not exercised, preliminary Air Force estimates indicate there will be at least a $700M cost impact above the current and projected contract cost to renegotiate similar capability scope to launch the remaining Block Buy contract missions (19 NSS satellites).

In addition, if there is an immediate ban on RD–180 engines for NSS Atlas V missions, the Air Force would have to remanifest already awarded Atlas V missions to the more expensive Delta IV (and in some cases the very expensive Delta Heavy) as SpaceX's Falcon 9 is not capable of lifting those missions leading to a 3–4 year delay in the launch manifest. An independent review led by Gen (ret) Mitchell, and later revalidated by the Air Force, estimated an overall cost increase of as much as $5.1B to accomplish this remanifesting. This "worst case scenario" cost estimate assumes an immediate loss of access to RD–180 engines. Thus, the estimate assumes no completion for the 37 Phase 1A and Phase 2 missions with a subset of these missions going to the more expensive Delta IV. In addition, the estimate includes the cost of procuring launch services on the Delta IV for the remaining Phase 1 Atlas V missions that have not launched and the delay cost associated with re-manifesting these missions. Last, the estimate includes the cost of maintaining the supporting infrastructure and workforce for Delta IV production and operational activity.

EFFECT ON DEFENSE POSTURE

30. Senator NELSON. What effect has uncertainty regarding the use of Russian-made engines had on our defense posture? What effect would continued uncertainty have going forward?

Secretary KENDALL. The deteriorating relationship with Russia has made it clear that continued use of Russian manufactured RD–180 engines to launch national security payloads is not in our Nation's best interest. Therefore, the Department is working vigorously to end our use of the RD–180 as soon as possible by supporting the development of new and improved launch service capabilities. The near-term loss of access to RD–180 engines would likely delay the launch of some of our critical national security payloads, which could impair the Department's ability to support the Warfighter in the field—clearly an unacceptable option. The sooner the Department can meet its goal of at least two commercially viable launch service capabilities, using domestically sourced propulsion systems that support all National Security Space requirements, the better for the Nation.

Secretary JAMES. The loss of assured access to space would be extremely damaging to national security. The challenge before us is to ensure space services continue to be available at the time and place of our choosing in an increasingly contested space domain. The first step in this process is to assure our ability to provide safe and reliable access to space for national security payloads. Uncertainty regarding its future availability results in increased risk to our national security space (NSS) posture.

QUESTIONS SUBMITTED BY SENATOR JEANNE SHAHEEN

SMALL BUSINESS

Senator SHAHEEN. I recently convened a meeting with my Small Business Advisory Council in New Hampshire and there were a number of issues raised that I would like to discuss. As you are aware, companies that do not win contract awards often protest the decision. The small businesses I talked to expressed concern with these numerous protests, as it causes delays and extra costs for their companies.

31. Under Secretary Kendall, how can we improve this process to lessen the adverse impact on smaller businesses?

Secretary KENDALL. I am also concerned about the increased protest impact on small businesses, as well as the toll it takes on the overall contracting process. Unfortunately, this is not an easy fix. It is within contractors' rights under the current legislation to protest a decision, without penalty, where the protest has no merit.

Senator SHAHEEN. One of the business owners I spoke with suggested charging the protesting company a fee of the total contract value, if a protest is denied.

32. Do you believe this would reduce the number of protests?

Secretary KENDALL. As stated in a prior answer, I am also concerned about the increased protest impact on small businesses, as well as the toll it takes on the overall contracting process. Unfortunately, this is not an easy fix. It is within contractors' rights under the current legislation to protest a decision, without penalty, where the protest has no merit. The Department would be willing to work with the Congress on measures that would discourage frivolous or speculative protests.

DOD

Senator SHAHEEN. In fiscal year 2014, the DOD spent more than $54 billion in prime contracts on small businesses, but fell short in in contracting with groups like women-owned small businesses. Had DOD reached the 5 percent goal of working with women-owned small businesses, $2.3 billion would have been awarded to these firms.

33. Can you tell me about the outreach DOD is doing to increase contracting subcontracting opportunities for women-owned small businesses?

Secretary KENDALL. I have charged the Acting Director of the Office of Small Business Programs, along with each of the Service Acquisition Executives, to keep up current momentum with our Small Business improvement over the last several years. The Department has set records for Small Business prime awards in three of the five categories for each of the previous two years, and I have no intention of slowing down small business initiatives. We are spearheading specific outreach for the two categories where the Department fell short during 2015, the HUBZone category and the Women-Owned Small Business category.

The Department was less than 0.6 percent away from meeting the Women-Owned Small Businesses (WOSB) goal and has improved steadily in this area over the past three years. The Department has participated in two WOSB-focused events and is working on initiatives utilizing Small Business Innovation Research to improve WOSB in technology contracts with the Department.

SBIR PROGRAM

Senator SHAHEEN. As you know, the SBIR program ensures that small businesses have an opportunity to conduct R&D for federal agencies, including Defense agencies. The program is up for reauthorization in 2017. On the Senate Small Business Committee, we recently held hearing on this issue so we can get started on a bill to make the program permanent, which would give the program stability for the agencies and the small business partners to develop technology.

34. In your view, does the SBIR program help defense agencies meet their technological needs?

Secretary KENDALL. Yes. The Small Business Innovation Research (SBIR) program is one of the Department's most valuable and impactful technology investment strategies and is an unquestionably vital initiative that should be made permanent for the Department. Its flexibility and agile buying process make the SBIR program highly effective.

One in four SBIRs reaches commercialization and is incorporated and used either directly for DOD and our sister agencies or in the commercial marketplace. For early stage technology investments, this is a high level of transition.

35. Senator SHAHEEN. Do you recommend permanent authorization for the SBIR and STTR programs?

Secretary KENDALL. Yes. The Small Business Innovation Research (SBIR) program and STTR are two of the Department's most valuable and impactful technology investment strategies and is an unquestionably vital initiative that should be made permanent for the Department.

One in four SBIR projects reaches commercialization and is incorporated and used either directly for DOD and our sister agencies or in the commercial marketplace. This success ratio is much higher than that of comparable commercial projects.

QUESTIONS SUBMITTED BY SENATOR JOE DONNELLY

SPACEX LAUNCH FAILURE INVESTIGATION REVIEW

Senator DONNELLY. In June 2015 SpaceX experienced a launch failure. While SpaceX was not carrying a DOD payload at the time, I understand the Air Force monitored the investigation following the failure and is conducting an independent review of the data and findings.

36. When do you expect to complete that review?

Secretary JAMES. The Air Force was an observer to the Federal Aviation Administration (FAA) and SpaceX-led investigation. The Space and Missile Systems Center (SMC) independent review is executing its standard mission assurance processes to determine root cause and corrective actions. These include assessment of the FAA and SpaceX investigation, additional analysis and test, and assessment of corrective actions. This independent assessment was completed on 31 March 2016. It will be staffed through Department stakeholders by the end of May 2016. Meanwhile, SpaceX remains certified and eligible to win an award for National Security Space launches.

Senator DONNELLY. The FAA and SpaceX completed their investigation last fall. NASA completed their independent review of the investigation late last year.

37. Why is the Air Force review is taking longer?

Secretary JAMES. The Air Force was an observer to the Federal Aviation Administration (FAA) and SpaceX-led investigation. The Space and Missile Systems Center (SMC) independent review is executing its standard mission assurance processes to determine root cause and corrective actions. These include assessment of the FAA and SpaceX investigation, additional analysis and test, and assessment of corrective actions. This independent assessment was completed on 31 March 2016. It will be staffed through Department stakeholders by the end of May 2016. Meanwhile, SpaceX remains certified and eligible to win an award for National Security Space launches.

LOSS OF ATLAS V

38. Senator DONNELLY. What are the implications of phasing Atlas V out of the U.S. launch vehicle inventory and relying on just Falcon 9 and Delta IV? How would this impact relative cost to the taxpayer and the ability to meet the launch schedule?

Secretary JAMES. A majority of the launch services provided by United Launch Alliance (ULA) use the Atlas V launch family, the more cost competitive of ULA's two launch product offerings. Therefore, ULA has not maximized the throughput for the Delta IV family. It will take time and funding to increase manufacturing capability to support an increased number of launches, resulting in launch delays. These delays will lead to increased satellite storage costs and additional costs to counter obsolescence issues associated with the Delta IV vehicle.

In addition to these assessed costs, Tori Bruno, CEO of ULA, publicly stated, during the HASC Strategic Forces Subcommittee hearing on June 26, 2015, that it costs 35 percent more to build a Delta IV launch vehicle than an Atlas V. Based on initial estimates, it would cost DOD in excess of $1.5B more to implement a Falcon 9 and Delta IV only approach for Evolved Expendable Launch Vehicle (EELV) Phase 2 (launch procurement in fiscal year 2018–2022).

39. Senator DONNELLY. Please describe the additional cost for a Delta IV launch vehicle and the cost of launch, compared to an Atlas V.

Secretary JAMES. Any costs associated with the Delta IV and Atlas V launch vehicles are ULA Proprietary. However, Tori Bruno, CEO of ULA, publicly stated at the HASC Strategic Forces Subcommittee hearing on June 26, 2015 that it costs 35 percent more to build a Delta IV launch vehicle than an Atlas V. Based on initial estimates, it would cost DOD in excess of $1.5B more to implement a Falcon 9 and Delta IV only approach for Evolved Expendable Launch Vehicle (EELV) Phase 2 (launch procurement in fiscal year 2018–2022).

40. Senator DONNELLY. Is industry on the proper path to replace the RD–180 within the time criteria set forth in statute?

Secretary KENDALL. The Department wants to end use of the RD–180 as soon as possible but does not believe this can be accomplished before 2021 or 2022. To be clear, the Department does not intend to unilaterally pay for the development of a direct replacement engine for the RD–180 on the Atlas V. The costs would be excessive to the Department, and a specific engine program would only benefit one launch service provider.

The Department's goal is competitive public-private partnerships with commercial launch service providers that result in new and improved launch service capabilities. This is the quickest and most efficient way to get off the RD–180.

41. Senator DONNELLY. In your view, how much longer should RD–180 equipped Atlases be allowed to fly?

Secretary KENDALL. The Department wants to end use of the RD–180 as soon as possible but does not believe this can be accomplished without significantly impacting operational requirements before 2021 or 2022. If new or improved launch service capabilities are certified before that time, the Department will transition to them as soon as they are available.

RD–180 AVAILABILITY

Senator DONNELLY. Discussion of the RD–180 issue often assumes that a ready supply of RD–180 engines are available for import on short notice.

42. Can you briefly describe the timing of RD–180 imports? For example, how far in advance of use must they be ordered?

Secretary JAMES. United Launce Alliance (ULA) orders RD–180s two years in advance of our normal Launch Vehicle Production Services (LVPS) order timeline. ULA orders are based on forecasted commercial and Government sales, and they procure in advance to achieve economic order quantities. According to ULA, how far in advance varies depending on a number of factors, such as inventories, Atlas launch rates, etc.

Senator DONNELLY. It has been suggested that ULA created an artificial shortage of RD–180s by not setting aside five engines delivered prior to the invasion of Crimea for national security purposes.

43. Did ULA approach the Air Force and offer to sell the five RD 180s already committed to those missions?

Secretary JAMES. No, ULA did not approach the Air Force to purchase RD–180s because management of the RD–180 engines is based on ULA internal business practices. The Government procures launch services from ULA. ULA is in the best position to provide detailed information regarding the timing of ULA's assignment of RD–180 engines.

44. Senator DONNELLY. Of the missions these five RD–180s have been obligated to, how many support U.S. national security objectives?

Secretary JAMES. It is the Government's understanding that two of these RD–180's are being utilized for National Security Space (NSS) launch missions.

RD–180 REPLACEMENT

45. Senator DONNELLY. Setting aside cost, what is the quickest, most reliable path for the U.S. to eliminate its dependence on the RD–180? Please explain.

Secretary JAMES. U.S. Government support for a robust and diverse industrial base that can deliver safe and reliable National Security Space (NSS) launch services at a competitive price is central to assuring access to space. A strategy of shared investment with industry using public-private partnerships to develop new and/or upgraded launch services is absolutely imperative because it ensures industry shares some of the cost burden and responsibility for success, offers the best chance of solving technical challenges and provides the opportunity to harness industry's creative ideas in ways to achieve propulsion and launch system performance requirements. Following the Rocket Propulsion System investments we are making with fiscal year 2015 and fiscal year 2016 funds, we plan to quickly shift towards an investment in one or more new or upgraded launch systems that can provide launch services to the NSS community. The goal is two or more domestic, commercially viable launch service providers that also meet NSS launch needs as quickly as possible, and it is the DOD's position that public-private partnerships are the quickest, most reliable path to meet that goal.

QUESTIONS SUBMITTED BY SENATOR MARTIN HEINRICH

RESPONSIVE LAUNCH

Senator HEINRICH. The Air Force has expressed its support for concepts such as "disaggregation" and "rapid reconstitution" that require new, more flexible, launch architectures. ORS experimented with such an approach last year with Super Strypi. An investigation is under way to determine what went wrong with that experimental launch.

46. Is the Air Force still committed to developing low-cost launch capabilities?

Secretary JAMES. The Air Force is committed to lowering launch cost while maintaining mission assurance and providing assured access to space for validated operational requirements across the entire range of payload classes. The Air Force's Space and Missile Systems Center has two procurement initiatives currently in progress to maintain and expand access to the maturing small launch market as a complement to the AF's large launch capability. The Small Rocket Program (SRP)-4 is in development to add a 0–400 lb. to low earth orbit capability to a contract which has traditionally been used only for sounding rockets and targets, and we expect Super Strypi and others to compete for this multiple-award contract. Similarly, the rideshare/data for boosters initiative seeks to utilize an existing GSA schedule contract to procure cost-effective rideshare services on a range of commercial launch missions, including both small and large launch vehicles. The Air Force approach to the low cost, responsive aspects of launch is further documented in the Operationally Responsive Low-Cost Launch Report to Congress from June 2015.

Secretary KENDALL. The Air Force is continually exploring new development opportunities such as Super Strypi, Small Business Innovation Research activities, and rideshare opportunities. The Air Force's Space and Missile Systems Center has two procurement initiatives currently in progress to maintain and expand access to the maturing small launch market as a complement to the Air Force's large launch capability. The Small Rocket Program-4 in development will add an up to 400 lb low earth orbit capability, and we would expect the Super Strypi to compete on this contract. Similarly, the Rideshare/Data for Boosters initiative seeks to utilize an existing General Services Administration schedule contract to procure cost-effective rideshare services on a range of commercial launch missions, including both small and large launch vehicles.

Senator HEINRICH. The small launch industry has the potential to play an important role in the future of military launches. There are over 15 American companies developing small satellite launch vehicles that can put payloads under 2,000 pounds into orbit. These small launch systems have the capacity to reduce launch costs and increase access to space.

47. What forms of low-cost launch is the Air Force exploring beyond Super Strypi, and how does Air Force plan to partner with industry in developing these innovative concepts?

Secretary JAMES. The Air Force is reaching out to the rapidly changing small launch industry on several fronts for low-cost launch capabilities. This includes planning for the future Small Rocket Program (SRP)-4 contract in support of future Super Strypi and other new small launch vehicle designs, small launch Small Business Innovation Research activities to foster development of the most promising technologies, and expanding rideshare opportunities such as Operationally Responsive Space (ORS)-6 and Data for Boosters. Additionally, the Air Force is a willing customer for commercial rideshare opportunities as an outgrowth of industry's efforts to develop small satellite launch vehicles.

Secretary KENDALL. The Air Force is reaching out to the rapidly changing small launch industry on several fronts for low-cost launch capabilities. This includes planning for the future Small Rocket Program-4 contract and working with industry on the future of Super Strypi and other new small launch vehicle designs. It also includes small launch Small Business Innovation Research activities intended to foster development of the most promising technologies, and expanding rideshare opportunities, such as Operationally Responsive Space-6 and the Data for ICBM Boosters initiative.

○

www.ingramcontent.com/pod-product-compliance
Lightning Source LLC
Chambersburg PA
CBHW080815280726
48660CB00018B/3465